The
529 Handbook

Maximize Your College Savings

David Spigarelli

Introduction

E ach year more and more students head to college. In September 2021, 19.8 million undergraduate students began their first year of college.[1] New college students are filled with excitement and are perhaps even a little nervous. Meanwhile, their parents feel dread and anxiety, concerned about how they're going to afford college. Students and parents alike hope to finish school without sinking in a sea of debt.

According to the College Board, the average tuition at a public four-year in-state university during the 2021-2022 school year was $10,740.[2] Out-of-state students experienced an even higher average tuition: $27,500. And students at private colleges faced the highest: $38,070. Multiplied by four years, the total tuition bill could be anywhere between $40,000 and $150,000.[3]

Tuition is only part of the cost of college. Education expenses include room and board, books, supplies, computer equipment, and personal expenses. Assuming your student doesn't live at home, the cost of four years of room and board can be as much as $50,000.[4] Add an additional $4,000 to cover books, supplies, a computer, transportation, and personal expenses. Your student's total cost for a four-year college degree could be easily more than $100,000.

Many students qualify for financial aid, but it rarely covers every expense. Most families end up bearing some portion of the cost.

What is a 529?

A 529[5] is a tax-advantaged investment account designed for college savings. Even though you don't receive an immediate federal income tax break for contributing to a 529, you do receive tax-free growth and tax-free withdrawals. Your home state may give you a tax break when you contribute.

Anyone can contribute to a 529, regardless of income. You can use your 529 at any accredited school, including most four- and two-year colleges, graduate and professional schools, and even many international schools. Not only can you use a 529 to pay tuition and fees, but you can also use a 529 to pay for room and board, books, supplies, computer equipment, and special needs services.

This book contains tips and tricks that could save you thousands of dollars using a 529.

Who is this book intended for?

This book is intended for individuals responsible for shouldering college expenses. Often that means the parents, but this book can also help students funding their own education or grandparents and relatives who want to help. With recent rules changes, even former students paying off student loans, or families enrolling their children in private K-12 schools can benefit. Even if your student receives a full-tuition scholarship or significant financial aid, you'll find tips that can save you money using a 529.

This book can help anyone with education-related expenses.

For many families, college is considered an important step in setting a child up for future success. However, don't lose sight of your own needs, particularly your own retirement.

If you aren't already taking advantage of workplace retirement plans (e.g., 401(k), 403(b), etc.) and individual retirement accounts, you should consider prioritizing doing so over saving for college. Contributing to tax-advantaged accounts can even increase your financial aid prospects. And if you have an employer that matches your contributions, you should prioritize contributing at least enough to get the full match before you start saving for college.

Remember, no one will loan you money for retirement.

Who am I?

I opened my first 529 savings account in 2006. Over the next sixteen years, I opened 529 accounts for each of my six children. I began putting my first 529 savings account to work a few years ago when my oldest daughter started college. I've both saved and spent using my 529s. Over time, I've learned the most efficient ways to use a 529 account for college. I am a software engineer, not a financial planner. I'm in the trenches with you, learning through experience, just like many other parents of college-bound students.

How to Read This Book

This book is divided into two parts. In Part 1, you'll estimate your college expenses, find the 529 plan that maximizes your savings, and then learn how to use your 529 to pay for college. You can think of Part 1 as the "happy path" traveled by most students and families using a 529. These chapters are of interest to all savers.

In Part 2, I dive into advanced topics and less common scenarios. You can focus on or skip sections of the book, depending on your situation:

- Everyone can benefit from reading the list of tips and strategies in *Chapter 11: Tips and Strategies*.

- If you're a high income earner and you suspect that you won't qualify for financial aid, you can skip both *Chapter 6: Scholarships, Grants, and Tax Credits* and *Chapter 7: 529s and Financial Aid*.

- If you don't plan on using any other methods to save for college except a 529, you can skip *Chapter 8: Other Ways to Save for College*.

- If you're a grandparent saving for a grandchild, see the sections on *Gift Tax and Generation Skipping Transfer Tax* and *Superfunding a 529* in Chapter 10.

- If you're worried about saving too much, see *Excessive Withdrawals* in Chapter 10.

- If you're worried you won't be able save enough, or maybe even at all, make sure you read *Maximizing State Tax Breaks Using Last-Minute Contributions* in Chapter 3.

Throughout the book, I provide examples that illustrate how 529s work. All of the students and families are fictional and any resemblance to actual persons, living or dead, is purely coincidental.

At the end of the chapters, you can find "Take Action!" steps that are designed to help you overcome both the inertia of inaction and the anxiety of action. You'll have more success if you take action as you read.

Disclaimer

Now for what this book is not.

I've worked hard to research the various federal and state laws and to cover every aspect of 529s as accurately as possible. However, both the federal and state rules about 529s change frequently. Neither I nor the publisher make any representation or warranty to the accuracy of the material in this book, nor to this book's adequacy or appropriateness for any purpose.

While this book contains financial information, it is not intended as a substitute for personalized advice from a professional financial advisor. Purchasing this book does not create a client relationship or other advisory, fiduciary, or professional service relationship with the publisher or with the author. You alone bear the responsibility of assessing the merits, risks, and suitability of the information contained in this book for your personal situation. Nothing in this book should be construed as financial advice.

Please keep in mind that any investment, including investments in a 529 account, can result in a partial or complete loss.

If you find any inaccuracies or if you have feedback on how this book could be better, I'd love to hear from you! I'd also love to hear how this book has helped you. You can reach me by email at: info@529handbook.com or through my website at https://529handbook.com.

---

[1] https://nces.ed.gov/programs/digest/d20/tables/dt20_105.30.asp

[2] https://research.collegeboard.org/trends/student-aid

[3] And hope that your student doesn't take longer!

[4] From the same College Board study, the average ranged from $11,950 (public) to $13,620 (private) in the 2021-2022 school year

[5] Officially, "qualified tuition program" (QTP); the nickname "529" comes from where they are defined in the law; see https://uscode.house.gov/view.xhtml?req=(title:26%20section:529%20edition:prelim)

Part 1

The Happy Path

1

Dispelling 529 Myths

As you learn about 529s and start saving for college, you'll find that many savers misunderstand 529s and how they can help when saving for college. This chapter debunks common myths and misconceptions that you may hear on your 529 journey.

Myth: I'll lose my 529 savings if my child doesn't go to college.

False. The money that you contribute to your 529 is safe from tax and penalties, even if you don't use it for college. You can learn about taxes and penalties in *Excessive Withdrawals* (in Chapter 10).

Myth: 529s can only be used for tuition.

False. You can use your 529 for tuition and fees, but also for room and board, books, supplies, and even computer equipment. You can also use your 529 to pay for trade school or registered apprenticeships. You can find out more about how to use your 529 in *Using Your 529* (Chapter 5).

Myth: If my student receives a scholarship or grant, my 529 is useless.

False. You can use your 529 regardless of whether your student received a scholarship or grant. You can learn how 529s are affected by scholarships and grants in *Scholarships, Grants, and Tax Credits* (Chapter 6).

Myth: I will lose control of the 529 when my student becomes an adult.

False. Unlike other saving methods, the account owner is always in control of how a 529 is used, not the beneficiary. You can learn more about how 529s compare with other ways to save in *Other Ways to Save for College* (Chapter 8).

Myth: My student is too old for a 529.

False. 529s don't have age limits. Whether it's a new baby or a 55 year-old going to graduate school, no student is too old to benefit from a 529. You can find more rules about opening a 529 in *Opening Your 529 Account* (Chapter 4).

Myth: I can only use my home state's 529 plan.

False. No matter which state you live in, you can always open a 529 in different state. You can learn more about how to find the right 529 plan for you in *Which 529 Plan is Best for Me?* (Chapter 3).

Myth: I won't qualify for financial aid if I use a 529.

False. Your 529 will be treated the same as your checking account in financial aid calculations. Learn more about how 529s impact financial aid in *529s and Financial Aid* (Chapter 7).

Myth: My income is too high to use a 529.

False. Anyone can use a 529, regardless of income. Learn more about who can open or contribute to a 529 in *Opening Your 529 Account* (Chapter 4).

Myth: Only rich families benefit from using 529s.

False. State tax breaks and tax-free growth help families at all income levels. Even if a student receives a generous grant or scholarship, a 529 can be used for expenses not covered by the grant or scholarship, including room and board, books, supplies, or a computer. Learn more about how to coordinate 529s with scholarships and grants in *Scholarships, Grants, and Tax Credits* (Chapter 6).

Myth: I can use the same 529 account for multiple children.

Partially true. You can change beneficiaries to move a 529 between children. But changing a beneficiary can be a hassle and there are limits on how frequently you can do so. Save yourself a headache and open a separate account for each child. Learn more about changing beneficiaries in *Changing Beneficiaries* (Chapter 10).

Myth: It's too late for me to save for college with a 529.

False. Many states give tax breaks for contributions, even if your student is in the final year of high school. Even after college, you can use a 529 to help pay off student loans. Learn more about state tax breaks in *Does Your Home State Offer a 529 Tax Break?* (Chapter 3). and using 529s to pay off student loans in *Student Loan Repayment* (Chapter 9).

Myth: A 529 can only be used at state schools in my home state.

False. You can use your 529 at any school that accepts federal student loan money. Learn more about eligible institutions in *Eligible Educational Institutions* (Chapter 5).

Myth: Only parents can use 529s.

False. A 529 can be opened by anyone, including grandparents, aunts, uncles, distant relatives, friends, and even the student themself. Learn more about the rules on opening and contributing to 529s in *Opening Your 529 Account* (Chapter 4).

Myth: It doesn't matter which 529 plan I use.

False. Using the wrong 529 plan can mean forfeiting significant state tax breaks or being saddled with high fees. Discover how to find the right 529 for you in *Which 529 Plan is Best for Me?* (Chapter 3).

Myth: I can invest my 529 in anything I want.

False. 529 plans have limited investment options. You can't use them to invest in individual stocks, bonds, real estate, or exotic investments–such as gold or cryptocurrency. Learn more about how 529s compare with other ways to save in *Other Ways to Save for College* (Chapter 8).

Myth: I can switch my investments whenever I want.

False. The IRS allows you to change your investment options two times each year. Learn how 529s compare with other college saving methods in *Other Ways to Save for College* (Chapter 8).

2

Making a College Savings Plan

B efore jumping into the details of 529s, we need to make a college savings plan. Your plan will give you an idea of how much college can cost, and a target for how much you'll want to save using your 529. Saving too little has negative consequences, but so does saving too much. Making a plan will help you find the right balance.

Until your student's first day of class, there are going to be a lot of unknowns. Your initial plan won't be completely accurate–but it doesn't need to be. Even a rough plan can help as you begin saving. Your plan consists of answering two questions: what is the advertised price for college, and what is the actual cost that you'll be expected to pay? After answering these two questions, you'll better understand how much you'll need to save, borrow, or earn to pay for college.

What Is the Advertised Price of College?

The first step in making a plan is to determine the advertised cost of college. Few students actually end up paying the advertised price, but starting there will help you know the maximum amount that you could end up paying for college.

The advertised price depends on where your student attends school. If your student is only a few years away from college, you may already have an idea of where they'll attend. If you have a hard time answering this question, no worries. Simply start with a school you are familiar with or a public university in your home state. Don't worry if your student doesn't actually end up attending the school in your plan. You can always adjust your plan when you have a better idea of where they'll attend.

> **Example:** Ann lives in Virginia. Her saving plan assumes that her twelve-year-old daughter, Jill, will attend Virginia Tech, just like she did. Even if Jill attends a different school, Ann is confident that her college expenses won't change much.

Schools that accept federal student aid are required to publish an official "cost of attendance" (COA).[1] The COA is an estimate of how much a freshman undergraduate student can expect to pay during their first year. The COA includes obvious expenses, such as tuition, fees, and books, but it also includes expenses like room and board, transportation, and typical personal expenses. The COA is the advertised price of college, but many students end up paying less.

You can find your school's COA by searching online for "[name of school] cost of attendance." Many schools publish online calculators that can make this process easier. You can typically find them by searching for "[name of school] net price calculator." However, these calculators are often outdated.

> **Example:** Ann searches online for "Virginia Tech net price calculator" and finds a website that helps her estimate the cost of a four-year degree at Virginia Tech in 2022. The estimate includes tuition, fees, books and supplies, room and board, transportation, and personal expenses.

Fixed versus Discretionary Expenses

Not every college expense is equal. Once you've selected your school, you won't have much control over tuition or fees. These are fixed costs, set by your university. While you can use scholarships and grants to lessen their impact, you won't have control to change them.

Even though the cost for books and supplies is highly variable, you'll want to consider them as fixed costs. You shouldn't compromise your student's education by not buying a required textbook.

At a minimum, you should save enough in your 529 to cover these fixed costs, even if your student ends up receiving scholarships or grants. I'll cover more about how scholarships and grants impact 529s in *Scholarships, Grants, and Tax Credits* (Chapter 6).

> **Example:** In 2021, Virginia Tech's tuition and fees amount to $13,750. Together with the estimated books and supplies, Ann's fixed costs are $14,850. Ann makes a goal to save at least four times this amount in her 529.

Discretionary expenses include: where your student lives, what they eat, how they get to and from school, and any personal expenses. Unlike fixed expenses, you do have some control over discretionary expenses. Even though your college estimates what they think your student's needs are, there's certainly no penalty for underspending! I cover which expenses you can use your 529 to pay for in *Qualified Education Expenses* (Chapter 5).

The cost of attendance (COA) is the sum of both fixed and discretionary expenses, and is the maximum amount you should plan to save. You can't withdraw more from your 529 than the COA without paying income tax and penalties.

> **Example:** In 2021, Virginia Tech estimated a new freshman would pay $10,110 for room and board. Ann also budgets $1,000 for a computer for Jill's first year.
>
> Four years at Virginia Tech is $99,840.[2] Ann makes a goal to save $96,000 to pay for Jill's school.

What Will I Actually Pay for College?

Like many parents and students, after seeing the numbers in this chapter, you may be in shock. You may be wondering how you're ever going to afford college. Don't be discouraged! Many families receive financial aid, including grants, scholarships, in-state tuition, tax breaks, legacy discounts, loans, and income from work-study jobs.

If you knew how much aid your student would receive, you could lower your savings target. While the net price calculators estimate financial aid, it will be impossible to know exactly how much aid you'll receive until your student receives their financial aid award letter.

The great news is that you can skip this step, if you want! Because the current 529 rules don't punish you for your financial aid fortunes, you can simply assume no financial aid and aim for the full savings target. You can learn more about how scholarships, grants, and tax breaks affect 529s in Chapter 6.

While financial aid can include loans and income from work-study programs, those don't impact your 529.

Example: Using the net price calculator for Virginia Tech, Ann sees that Jill could qualify for $2,045 in grants and scholarships each year that she is in school. Ann's net cost of college for one year is reduced to $23,915. While Ann could use this new number as her maximum savings target, she could also ignore it. Either way, her use of her 529 won't be impacted.

Start Saving!

Armed with a savings target, you can determine how much you need to start saving today. The earlier you start saving, the more time your money has to grow.

To illustrate the power of compounding, take a simple example. Imagine you have a savings goal of $20,000 and your savings grow by an annual average rate return of 7%. If you only had two years to hit your goal, you'd need to save $779 every month![3] You would have contributed 93% of your goal, or $18,696.

If you instead had eighteen years to save up, you'd only need to save $46 each month to reach your goal.[4] You would have contributed only $9,936, or about 50% of your savings goal. That's the power of compounding!

Choose a savings goal somewhere between your minimum and your maximum savings targets for one year of college. Assuming your student will be done with college in four years, multiply your one-year savings goal by four. Then, project that into the future. Turning to the internet, search for "compound savings calculator," enter your savings target, a reasonable annual rate of return, and how many years your student has until college. Some calculators include inflation for a more accurate estimate.

> **Example:** Ann's minimum savings target is $14,850 and her maximum target is $25,960. She expects that Jill will live in the dorms during her first year but will live off campus in subsequent years, saving some money. Ann chooses an annual savings target of $24,000. She multiples this by four years for a savings target of $96,000.
>
> Ann thinks her college expenses will increase by an inflation rate of 2.5% each year during the six years before Jill starts college. Ann projects a savings target of $111,331.[5] Ann will need to start saving $1,435 each month to reach her target.[6]

Ann repeats the process for two other universities that she thinks Jill may attend: James Madison University and Penn State University

Summary

You've learned how to find the advertised price of college and how to budget fixed and discretionary expenses. You've calculated both minimum and maximum savings targets and made a savings goal.

In the next chapter, we'll find the 529 plan that will work best for your situation. Before reading on, take these action steps:

Take Action!

Total Time: 20 to 30 minutes

1. Write down a school that you think your student might attend

2. Using the school you chose, do an internet search for "[name of school] net price calculator"

    a. Fill out the calculator as accurately as possible

    b. Fill out the worksheet using the results of the calculator

    c. Repeat the process for another one or two schools

3. Armed with your net price, search the internet for "savings goal calculator." Choose a reasonable rate of return and see how much money you need to start saving each month to reach your goal. Enter your goal into the worksheet.

4. Pick a date halfway between now and the date your student will start college. Set a calendar reminder to check in with your plan on that date and make any needed adjustments.

College Savings Target Worksheet (Example)[7]

College	Virginia Tech	James Madison	Penn State
Non-Discretionary Expenses Only include: • Tuition • Fees • Books and supplies	Tuition & Fees $13,750 Books & supplies $1,100	Tuition & Fees $12,914 Books & supplies $1,098	Tuition & Fees $36,476 Books & supplies $1,840
Minimum Savings Target	**$14,850**	**$14,012**	**$38,316**
Discretionary Expenses Include: • Room & board • Computer Don't include personal or transportation costs	Room & board $10,110 Computer $1,000	Room & board $11,074 Computer $1,000	Room & board $12,318 Computer $1,000
Maximum Savings Target	**$25,960**	**$26,086**	**$51,634**
Non-Loan Financial Aid (optional)	$2,045	$5,297	$0
My One-Year Savings Goal	**$24,000**	**$24,000**	**$50,000**
My Four-Year Savings Goal	**$96,000**	**$96,000**	**$200,000**
Expected rate of return, after inflation	5% - 2.5% inflation = **2.5%** average annual rate of return		
How many years until college?	6 years before Jill starts college		
Monthly Savings Goal	**$1,437**	**$1,437**	**$2,994**

College Savings Target Worksheet

College			
Non-Discretionary Expenses Only include: • Tuition • Fees • Books and supplies	Tuition & Fees Books & supplies	Tuition & Fees Books & supplies	Tuition & Fees Books & supplies
Minimum Savings Target			
Discretionary Expenses Include: • Room & board • Computer Don't include personal or transportation costs	Room & board Computer	Room & board Computer	Room & board Computer
Maximum Savings Target			
Non-Loan Financial Aid (optional)			
My One-Year Savings Goal			
My Four-Year Savings Goal			
Expected rate of return, after inflation			
How many years until college?			
Monthly Savings Goal			

---

[1] https://uscode.house.gov/view.xhtml?
req=(title:20%20section:1087ll%20edition:prelim)

[2] ($14,850 for tuition and books + $10,110 for room and board) * 4
years, + $1,000 for a computer

[3] Excel formula: =pmt(7%/12,12*2,0,-20000)

[4] Excel formula: =pmt(7%/12,12*18,0,-20000)

[5] Excel formula: =fv(2.5%, 6, 0, -96000)

[6] Using the following Excel formula, Ann's present value is close to
zero: =pv(2.5%/12, 6*12, -1435, 111330)

[7] Links for COA and Net Price Calculators:

- Virginia Tech: https://finaid.vt.edu/undergraduate/coa.html;
  https://tcc.ruffalonl.com/
  Virginia%20Polytechnic%20Institute%20and%20State%20Unive
  rsit/Freshman-Students

- James Madison: https://www.jmu.edu/financialaid/learn/cost-of-
  attendance-undergrad.shtml; https://www.jmu.edu/financialaid/
  calculators/undergraduate.shtml

- Penn State: https://admissions.psu.edu/costs-aid/tuition/; https://
  cce.ais.psu.edu/netprice-calculator/

Excel formulas for Monthly Savings Goals: =PMT(2.5%/12, 12*6,
96000), =PMT(2.5%/12, 12*6, 96000) and =PMT(2.5%/12, 12*6,
200000)

3

Which 529 Plan is Best for Me?

Now that you've taken a peek at how much you'll want to save for college, let's find the 529 plan that works best for you and your situation.

When choosing a 529 plan, consider the following questions:

- Does your home state offer a tax break for 529 contributions?

- Do you prefer using a financial advisor or doing it yourself?

- Do you prefer a prepaid option over a savings option? Or one of each?

- Are the investment options sufficient?

- Are the plan fees or investment expenses low?

- Are you happy with the experience (e.g., customer service, website, familiar firm, etc.)?

Does Your Home State Offer a 529 Tax Break?

More than thirty states provide a state tax break when contributing to a 529. Most states require that you participate in the home state plan to receive the tax break. However, as of 2021, seven states give the tax break regardless of which plan you use. Any tax break should make it worth it to use your home state plan.

Tax Breaks By State[1]

States that offer a tax break when contributing to any 529, including out-of-state plans:		
• Arizona	• Minnesota	• Pennsylvania
• Arkansas	• Missouri	
• Kansas	• Montana	

States that offer a tax break when contributing to the in-state 529 plan:		
• Alabama	• Louisiana	• Oklahoma
• Colorado	• Maryland	• Oregon
• Connecticut	• Massachusetts	• Rhode Island
• District of Columbia	• Michigan	• South Carolina
• Georgia	• Mississippi	• Utah
• Idaho	• Nebraska	• Vermont
• Illinois	• New Jersey	• Virginia
• Indiana	• New Mexico	• West Virginia
• Iowa	• New York	• Wisconsin
	• Ohio	

States with no tax breaks for 529 contributions:		
• Alaska	• Maine	• Tennessee
• California	• Nevada	• Texas
• Delaware	• New Hampshire	• Washington
• Florida	• North Carolina	• Wyoming
• Hawaii	• North Dakota	
• Kentucky	• South Dakota	

If your home state doesn't offer any tax breaks for 529 contributions, then you can pick an out-of-state plan with lower fees or better investment options. Feel free to skip the rest of this section.

Tax Break Limitations

Tax breaks for 529 contributions can vary widely by state. The tax breaks usually either reduce your taxable income (a deduction) or reduce your tax bill (a credit).

Examples of how rules can differ between states include:

- Some states limit the size of the tax break. Example: Indiana provides a maximum credit of $1,000 to joint filers.

- Some states limit who can receive the tax break. Example: New York only allows account owners or spouses (for joint filers) to deduct contributions.

- Some states give a tax break depending on the age of the beneficiary. Example: Utah gives a tax credit only if the beneficiary is under age 19.

- Some states restrict tax breaks by income. Example: Oregon requires higher earners to contribute more to receive the same benefit as lower earners.

- Some states limit tax breaks if you withdraw money. Example: Minnesota only gives a tax break if annual contributions exceed withdrawals.

- If you contribute more than the annual limit, some states allow you to roll the excess contribution into future tax years, and other states don't. Example: In Arkansas, joint filers that contribute more than $10,000 in any year, can deduct the excess in future years. In Nebraska, joint filers can only deduct $10,000, but can't carry over any excess.

- And finally, some states will give you a tax break when you roll over a 529 account from another state's plan. Others won't. More on rollovers in *Rolling Over a 529 Plan* (Chapter 10).

It's difficult to overstate the impact of a state tax break. If your home state gives a tax break for participating in its plan, then you should prioritize contributing to your home state's 529 plan to maximize the tax break.

> **Example:** Anders lives in Nebraska with his two children. In 2022, his state income tax rate is 6.84%. He contributes $12,000, split between two Nebraska-sponsored Nest529 accounts.

Unfortunately, Nebraska limits his deduction to only $5,000 and disallows carrying the excess into future tax years. When he files his 2022 state income tax return, his total tax savings is $342. Anders could have maximized his tax break by splitting his contribution across tax years: contributing $5,000 in 2022, another $5,000 in 2023, and the remaining $2,000 in 2024, for a total tax savings of $821.

If your state's tax break is capped, consider contributing at least the bare minimum to get the tax break, and then investing the excess in another state's 529 plan that has lower fees or better investment options.

> **Example:** Denzel lives in Oregon. To maximize his state tax break, Denzel contributes $1,500 to his 529 account, saving $150 in taxes. He invests his contribution in the US Equity option, which has a fee of 0.28%.
>
> Because Oregon's tax break is capped, Denzel contributes an additional $4,000 to a California 529 account, investing his contribution in a similar option that has a lower fee: 0.06%. Repeating this every year, Denzel will have saved $695 in fees when his daughter leaves for college.[2]

Maximizing State Tax Breaks Using Last-Minute Contributions

Depending on your home state's 529 rules, it may make sense to pass every expense through your 529. For example, if a tuition bill comes due, you first make a contribution for the same amount to your 529, then immediately pay the bill using the 529. Making last-minute contributions in this way could earn you the state tax break.[3]

Example: Isabel lives in New Mexico, which has an unlimited state tax deduction for contributions to the home state plan. She hasn't been able to save anything for her son's college expenses. However, she opens a 529 account right before her son heads to college. Every time she has an education expense, Isabel first deposits money into her 529, then immediately withdraws the money to pay for the expense. During 2021, Isabel passed $10,450 through her 529, saving her $512 in state income tax.[4]

Later, Isabel moves to New Jersey. In January, her son received a $3,250 student loan and the loan proceeds are immediately applied to his tuition bill by the university.

In October, Isabel discovered that New Jersey began giving a state tax deduction in 2022. She immediately opened a 529 and contributed $3,250. A few days later, she withdrew the full amount and paid off the loan. When Isabel files her 2022 state income tax return, she deducts the $3,250 from her income, and saves $207 in state income tax.

Would You Rather Do It Yourself, or Use a Financial Advisor?

Most states offer a do-it-yourself or "direct-sold" 529 plan. You can open the account through either the plan website or by mailing in a form. These plans offer a limited set of investment options and often come with the lowest fees.

Some savers aren't comfortable with do-it-yourself solutions and prefer to work with a trusted financial advisor in navigating investment decisions. As of 2022, thirty states offered "advisor-sold" 529 plans that can only be accessed through a financial advisor. If you already have a financial advisor, they can help you set up your 529. Advisor-sold plans may come with more investment options, but they often come with higher fees.

If you use a financial advisor for your 529 investing and you live in a state with a 529 tax break, make sure you don't lose any tax break by using an out-of-state plan. Losing the tax break can cancel out any advantages of using an advisor.

> **Example:** Elise lives in Ohio and doesn't have a financial advisor. She opens a 529 account with Ohio's direct-sold CollegeAdvantage plan. She sets up recurring monthly contributions into the 2034 Portfolio target date fund, which has a .29% expense ratio.

Elise's neighbor, Ryan, already has a relationship with a financial advisor, who helps him set up a 529 account with Ohio's advisor-sold Ohio BlackRock CollegeAdvantage plan. Ryan's advisor also helps him set up recurring monthly contributions into the BlackRock College 2035 option, which has a 0.73% expense ratio, a fee that's two and half times higher than the equivalent, direct-sold option.

Do You Prefer a Prepaid Tuition Plan or a Savings Plan?

There are two types of 529 plans: prepaid tuition plans and savings plans. Each type comes with trade-offs. Which type of account is right for you depends on your individual preferences and situation.

Prepaid Tuition Plans

Prepaid tuition plans appeal to savers who are worried about affording escalating college expenses. Prepaid tuition plans allow you to buy future tuition credits at in-state colleges at today's rates. You can still use these plans for out-of-state and private schools, but your funds are first converted into cash using the current in-state tuition rate.

As of 2022, only nine states[5] offered prepaid tuition plans. Most prepaid tuition plans require either the account owner or the beneficiary to be residents. If you don't live in a state that offers a prepaid plan, then this option is likely not for you.

Advantages of prepaid tuition plans:

- Simplicity of investment options (there aren't any!)

- Tax-free withdrawals

- Keeping pace with escalating tuition rates

- May be guaranteed by the state

- May come with state income tax breaks, and

- Protection from market fluctuation.

Disadvantages include:

- Growth is limited to tuition increases. With a prepaid plan, you're still paying the full tuition bill, but at today's rates.

- If your student attends a private or out-of-state university, you may end up with less money than you expect after it's converted.

- Some prepaid tuition plans can only be used for tuition and fees. You may still need a separate 529 savings account to pay for room and board or for a computer.

- Contribution limits are generally smaller than savings plans and limits are often tied to in-state tuition rates.

- Some prepaid plans don't allow new accounts for beneficiaries who are seniors in high school or older.

- Prepaid plans often have limited enrollment windows.

- Funds may need to be used up by the time the beneficiary reaches a certain age.

   Example: Jing lives in Washington state and opened a prepaid tuition account for his newborn son. Since then, Jing has purchased 400 units, the equivalent of four years of tuition and fees at the University of Washington, Washington state's most expensive public university in 2021.

   When Jing started saving in 2004, in-state tuition and fees were just $5,286.[6] By 2021, tuition and fees had increased to $12,076, a 5% average annual increase.[7] Jing's average cost per unit was $82. He saved $15,504 by using the prepaid plan.[8]

The Private College 529 Prepaid Tuition Plan

In addition to prepaid tuition plans sponsored by states, there is one prepaid tuition plan sponsored by a group of almost 300 private schools.[9] The plan works by purchasing "tuition certificates" that can be used to pay tuition at participating schools. The value of a certificate depends on which school your student attends and in what year you purchased the certificate.

Disadvantages include:

- If your student doesn't attend a participating school, you can request a refund. However, the refundable value is capped at a maximum 2% annual growth from when you purchased the certificate. Learn how to avoid taxes and penalties by rolling any refund into another 529 in *Tuition Refunds* (Chapter 10).

- Tuition certificates can only be used for tuition. You'll need a separate savings plan to cover room and board, books, supplies, and a computer.

Example: Michael opens a Private College 529 Plan, hoping his daughter will be accepted to either Massachusetts Institute of Technology or Boston University. Michael has purchased enough certificates to pay 87% of the cost of MIT's tuition and 86% of the cost of BU, regardless of future tuition increases at either school.

Unfortunately, Michael's daughter doesn't get accepted to either school. Instead, she attends a different in-state school. When Michael requests a refund, a tuition certificate that he paid $1,000 for in 2012 is refunded to him as $1,219.[10] If Michael had instead invested in the Total Market Index option of the Massachusetts-sponsored 529 plan, his same $1,000 could have been worth $3,730.[11]

529 Savings Plans

As of 2022, nearly every state offers at least one 529 savings plan. These plans work like a workplace 401(k) retirement account: you contribute money and then choose how your contribution is invested from a limited set of options that usually include both passive (index) and actively managed funds. The value of the account rises and falls depending on which option you chose. When you withdraw money, the investments are turned into cash at the current market rate.

Most 529 savings plans allow out-of-state participants. If your state doesn't offer a tax break, you can choose another state's plan that offers better investment options or lower fees.

The advantages of a 529 savings account include:

- Contribution limits are generally much higher than prepaid plans

- You chose how it's invested from a fixed set of options, and

- If your investments do well, you can end up beating both inflation and tuition increases.

The disadvantages of a 529 savings account include:

- No guarantee. Your chosen investment option can underperform or even lose value, leaving you with less than you planned for.

- Even though most 529s have a small list of options, choosing how to invest can still be intimidating for many savers

The Best of Both Worlds

Both prepaid tuition plans and savings plans come with disadvantages. The great news is that you don't have to choose between them. Instead, you can open an account of both types. This gives you all of the benefits of both types, but can be more complex to manage.

Are the Investment Options Sufficient?

Unlike other types of investment accounts, you can't invest your 529 account in just any investment that you want. Like many workplace retirement accounts, 529 accounts come with a limited set of investment options. Plans typically include:

- **Target-enrollment funds:** These options target the year that the beneficiary will enter college. The further you are away from the target date, the more the fund invests in higher-risk, higher-reward options, such as stocks. As the target date gets closer, the fund shifts to lower-risk, lower-reward options, such as bonds. These funds often come with slightly higher fees than passive funds.

- **Actively managed mutual funds:** These funds are actively managed by a fund advisor and are often a mix of both stocks and bonds. They often come with the highest fees in order to compensate the fund advisor.

- **Passively managed mutual funds:** These funds are often called "index" funds because they track a market index. They often have the lowest fees because they don't need to pay a fund advisor to pick investments.

- **Principal preservation funds:** These funds sacrifice return in favor of lower risk investment options. While your account will never go down in value, your rate of return is usually a fraction of either the stock or bond options. Examples include FDIC-insured savings and certificates of deposits (CDs).

Even though 529 accounts come with fewer investment options than other college saving options, this isn't necessarily a disadvantage. Too many choices can be overwhelming. Ask yourself if the plan's options are sufficient and if they match your comfort level.

Does the Plan Have Low Fees?

After considering any state tax breaks and whether the plan's investment options are sufficient, you should next consider the plan's fees and expenses.

Account fees may include:

- **Enrollment or application fee:** A one-time fee to open your 529 account. As of 2022, virtually no direct-sold 529 plans have enrollment or application fees. It should be a red flag if a plan charges this fee.

- **Account maintenance fee:** An annual fee charged to the account owner. This fee is often waived if the account owner is a resident, has a large enough account balance, enrolls in electronic statements, or sets up a recurring contribution.

- **Program manager fee:** A percentage-based fee, usually applied to all investment options. This fee covers the plan manager's expenses.

- **State fee:** A percentage-based fee, usually applied to all investment options. This fee covers the state's expenses to sponsor the plan.

Investment expenses may include:

- **Investment sales charge:** A percentage-based fee charged by advisor-sold plans on every contribution. This fee compensates your financial advisor.

- **Investment expense ratio:** A percentage-based fee, charged by the manager of the investment option. This expense ratio varies between investment options within the same plan. This type of fee is usually invisible because it's baked into the investment's net asset value price, or NAV.

These are the most common fees. Each plan is different and may include other additional fees.

Example: Ashley is a resident of Idaho and contributes to an Idaho-sponsored IDeal 529 account. There was no fee to open the account, and because she is a resident, Ashley isn't charged the $20 monthly account maintenance fee. She invested her contributions in the age-based Aggressive Growth Portfolio (7-9), which has a total 0.49% expense ratio. The fee is composed of a 0.40% program manager fee, a 0.05% state fee, and a 0.04% investment expense ratio. Her account balance is $10,000 at the start of the year. In one year, her investment fees were $49, which she didn't notice because the fee was rolled into the investment option's price.

Fees and Investment Performance

Fees matter, especially when compounded over years. Consider Rafael, a resident of South Dakota, who started saving $50 per month when his daughter was born. South Dakota's plan has fees that are relatively higher than other plans. The investment option with the highest fee in South Dakota's direct-sold 529 plan is the Pimco All Asset option, which has an annual expense ratio of 1.19%.

Because South Dakota has no state tax break for contributions, Rafael decides to shop around. He sees that California's direct-sold 529 plan has an Index U.S. Equity Portfolio investment option with an annual expense ratio of 0.06%.

Consider the impact that these two fees could have on Rafeal's savings. Assume the two investment options both have an average annual rate of return of 5% and that Rafael contributes $50 each month for 18 years. By the time his daughter starts college, Rafael's account could be 12% bigger if he saved using the California option ($17,353) rather than the South Dakota option ($15,484).[12]

Plan Aesthetics and Experience

Other things you might consider as you evaluate 529 plans:

- Is the plan website easy to use? Does the plan have a reputation for good customer service?

- Do you already have a relationship with a financial firm that manages a 529? For example, Charles Schwab manages the 529 plan sponsored by Kansas. Fidelity manages 529 programs with five different states: Arizona, Connecticut, Delaware, Massachusetts, and New Hampshire. Other examples include: T. Rowe Price (Alaska), USAA (Nevada), and TD Ameritrade (Nebraska), to name a few.

Remember that while it's convenient to open an account at a firm that you already have a relationship with, it's not worth missing out on a tax break from your home state's plan.

If your home state gives a tax break for 529 contributions, you should probably hold your nose and look past any aesthetic problems.

> **Example:** Zane lives in Utah. He qualifies for a $105 state tax credit by contributing $2,130 (in 2022) to Utah's 529 plan. However, he chooses instead to open a 529 account through Vanguard, where he already has both IRA and brokerage accounts. Vanguard's 529 plan sponsor is Nevada. By not using his home state's 529 plan, he misses out on the state income tax credit.

Summary

You now have everything you need to find the 529 plan that is right for your student(s) and your situation. Before continuing to the next chapter, take these steps:

Take Action!

Total Time: 30 to 60 minutes

1. Find the website for your home state's 529 plan. You can start by either searching for "[home state] 529" or by going to https://www.collegesavings.org/find-my-states-529-plan/

2. Familiarize yourself with your state's 529 plan.

    a. Search for "[home state] 529 tax benefits". Does your home state offer a tax break for contributing to a 529 account? If so, how much? (Hint: if your state doesn't have income tax, you probably don't have a tax break, but there may be other benefits.)

    b. What restrictions does your home state plan have?

    c. Does your home state offer a prepaid tuition plan? A savings plan? Both?

    d. Find the investment options for your state's plan. Do they offer low-cost index funds? Target date funds?

Principal preserving options? Which investment option has the lowest fee? Which has the highest?

e. What fees does your home state's 529 plan have? Try searching for "[your home state] 529 fees."

f. How happy are you with the plan's website?

3. Using https://www.collegesavings.org, pick two or three other top 529 plans and compare them with your home state's plan.

a. If you need a suggestion of where to start, look at any of the following three plans, known for having some of the lowest fees and diversified index fund options:

- California's ScholarShare529[13]

- Utah's My529, and[14]

- Ohio's CollegeAdvantage.[15]

My home state 529:

Website:

- What tax breaks does my home state offer for 529 contributions?

- If my home state offers a prepaid option, would I prefer it to a savings option? Can the prepaid option be used for more than just tuition and fees?

- Which investment option in my home state plan has the lowest fee? Highest?

- Which investment options do I prefer?

- Does the plan offer target date funds or low-cost index funds?

Choose at least two or three top-ranked plans and compare them with your home state plan.

Alternate Plan #1:

Website:

- Does the plan offer target date funds or low-cost index funds?

- Which investment options do I prefer? How do their fees compare with the home state options?

Alternate Plan #2:

Website:

- Does the plan offer target date funds or low-cost index funds?

- Which investment options do I prefer? How do their fees compare with the home state options?

---

[1] As of April 2022; Arkansas gives a partial benefit if using another state's 529 plan

[2] Excel formula: =fv(0.28%, 13 years, $4,000, $0) - fv(0.06%, 13 years, $4,000, $0), or $695.02

[3] States where this strategy won't work include: Minnesota (the tax deduction is reduced by any withdrawals), Utah (the credit only applies if the beneficiary is younger than 19), and Wisconsin (the tax deduction is reduced by any withdrawals made in the previous 365 days)

[4] Top tax bracket in New Mexico is 4.9%

[5] In 2022, the following states offer prepaid tuition plans: Florida, Maryland, Massachusetts, Michigan, Mississippi, Nevada, Pennsylvania, Texas, and Washington

[6] Historic rates from http://depts.washington.edu/opbfiles/web/2016-17%20Tuition%20&%20Fee%20History.pdf

[7] Excel formula: =rate(2021-2004,0,-$5,286,$12,076)

[8] ($12,076 * 4) - ($82 * 400)

[9] 295 member schools as of the 2021-2022 school year; see https://www.collegewell.com/wp-content/uploads/2019/12/PC529_Pricing_Guide.pdf

[10] Excel formula: =fv(2%, 2022-2012, 0, -$1,000)

[11] Ten-year performance of the Total Market Index options, as of 3/31/2022, was 14.07%. Past performance is not a guarantee of future performance. See https://fundresearch.fidelity.com/mutual-funds/summary/MAXFSTMX6?appcode=529 for more details.

---

[12] Excel formulas: =fv((5%-0.06%)/12, 18 * 12, -50) and =fv((5%-1.19%)/12, 18 * 12, -50)

[13] https://www.scholarshare529.com/

[14] https://my529.org/

[15] https://www.collegeadvantage.com/

4

Opening Your 529 Account

In the last chapter, you found the 529 plan that works best for you and your situation. By the end of this chapter, you'll have gathered everything you need to open your account and start saving, including:

- Details about the account owner and beneficiary

- Where to open your account

- How to contribute to your account

- How to choose the right investment options, and

- What to expect at tax time.

Gathering Account Details

No matter which plan you choose for your 529, there are basic facts you'll need to have ready, including:

- Account owner's legal name, date of birth, address, and Social Security number (SSN) or Individual Taxpayer Identification number (ITIN). Usually the account owner is an individual, but some plans permit a trust to be the account owner. Remember that many states may only give tax breaks to the account owner.

- Beneficiary's legal name, date of birth, address, and SSN or ITIN. If you have more than one beneficiary, then you'll need to open an account for each beneficiary.

- Designated successor in case of the account owner's death. This can be anyone you trust, including a spouse, other relative, or even the beneficiary. If you don't specify a designated successor, depending on your plan's rules, it may default to the beneficiary.

- If you're making your initial contribution using direct debit, you'll need both the routing and account numbers for your checking or savings account.

Where Do I Open My 529 Account?

You can't simply walk into your local bank branch and open a 529 account. If you've chosen a do-it-yourself or "direct-sold" plan, you'll open your account by either using the plan's website that you found in *Which 529 Plan is Best for Me?* (Chapter 3) or mailing in your application. If instead you're using a financial advisor, work with them to open your account.

How Do I Contribute to My 529?

Your first contribution will happen when you first open your account, either by a direct withdrawal from your bank account, or by mailing a check. Unlike other popular investment account options, you cannot contribute using stocks, bonds, mutual funds, ETFs, or other investments into your 529 account. Contributions must be in cash or equivalent.

Most plans offer recurring contribution options, often with either very low or no minimums. Some plans even allow for payroll direct deposit. These options help you spread out your contribution and create a pattern of saving with little or no interaction from you.

Many plans also have "gift card" options, allowing family and friends to easily contribute to your 529 account on holidays, birthdays, or other special occasions. To find gifting options, search for "[your home state] 529 gift options." Be aware that there are third-party companies that sell 529 gifting services for a fee.

How Much Can I Contribute to My 529?

The federal government lets each plan set its own contribution limits. Most savings plans have a maximum contribution limit between $300,000 and $500,000. Prepaid tuition plans may place limits on how many tuition credits can be purchased and when they can be purchased.

If you're contributing more than $16,000 in a single year to the same beneficiary, you can learn more about gift tax limitations and superfunding a 529 in *Gift Tax and Generation Skipping Transfer Tax* (Chapter 10).

How do I Choose What to Invest in?

If you open a direct-sold 529 savings account, you'll be in the driver's seat in choosing how your contributions are invested. When selecting your investment options, ask yourself these questions:

- **What is my tolerance for risk?** Do sudden market drops stress me out, even if I have years before I'll need the money?

- **How much time do I have until I need the money?** If you don't need the money for ten years, then you may be able to stomach more stocks than bonds. On the other hand, if you need it next year, you might want to steer toward bonds or principal preserving options.

- **What are the option's investment fees?** Actively managed options typically have higher fees than do passive options. An actively managed option must outperform the equivalent passive option by at least the difference in fees to be worth the extra cost.

- **What is the option's past performance?** Most 529 plans report performances over the previous one, five, and ten years. Remember, past performance is not a guarantee of future performance.

Once you've answered these questions, consider how each type of investment option fits your personality and situation. You can read more about them in the previous chapter, in *Are the Investment Options Sufficient?* (Chapter 3):

- **Prepaid Tuition:** This option appeals to <u>savers who would rather not worry about escalating tuition rates or what the market will do</u>. Depending on your home state, this may or may not be an option.

- **Target Date/Enrollment:** You choose the fund based on the date that you expect your beneficiary will start college. This option is low maintenance and <u>appeals to savers who want set-and-forget simplicity</u>.

- **Passive Index Funds:** These funds track specific market indices, typically a stock, bond, or international index. It's up to you to find the right balance between options and make adjustments as needed. This option appeals to savers who want more control over their investment.

- **Actively Managed Funds:** These funds target particular levels of risk, such as aggressive (i.e., more stock, less bonds), moderate, and conservative (i.e., more bonds, less stock). This option appeals to savers who want more control over their investment.

- **Guaranteed Portfolios:** These portfolios appeal to investors who want the safety of government-issued bonds or FDIC-insured funds. By choosing this option, you're giving up potentially higher returns and possibly losing to inflation. In return, your account won't lose value. This option appeals to savers who will be using their 529 soon or worry about market risk.

Note: Regardless of which option you choose today, you can change it. However, the 529 rules prevent you from changing your investment option more than twice a year. Individual 529 plans may place additional restrictions on how frequently you can change your investment.

Tax Time

When you contribute to a 529 account, you don't report anything on your federal income tax return. If your state gives a tax break for contributing, you'll report your contributions when filing your state tax return. Typically, the tax breaks are either a deduction from your taxable income or a tax credit. To get the details on your home state's tax break, just search "[home state] 529 tax benefit."

Summary

You have everything you need to open your first 529. Take these action steps today:

Take Action!

Total Time: 25 to 30 minutes

1. Fill out the attached worksheet with your account details for each account you are going to open

   a. Review your savings goal from *Making a College Savings Plan* (Chapter 2). How much will you contribute today and how much will you contribute each month?

2. Once you've answered the questions above, your next step is to open your first 529 account. Create your account and start saving!

529 Account Details   #_____

Login Username/Email & Password: _____/_____

Account Owner

- Legal name:
- Address:
- Date of Birth:
- SSN or ITIN: #_____

Beneficiary

- Legal name:
- Address:
- Date of Birth:
- SSN or ITIN: #_____

Designated Successor:

Bank Account

- Routing #:   #_____
- Account #:   #_____

Initial Contribution $_____

Monthly Contribution $_____

Investment Option:

- Target Date Fund –
  Year Graduating from High School   _____
- Option #1:   _____%
- Option #2:   _____%

5

Using Your 529

No matter how far into the future your college expenses are, be it months from now or even years, it's important to understand what will happen when you put your 529 to work. This chapter covers the details on what expenses qualify under the 529 rules, how to withdraw your money, and what you can expect at tax time. Understanding how to use a 529 can give you confidence on your journey and help you avoid pitfalls along the way.

Qualified Expenses

You can use your 529 to pay for any of the following expenses:

- **Tuition,** likely your largest education-related expense.

- **Mandatory fees, books, supplies, and equipment** required by the university or college.

- **Room and board** for students that are enrolled at least half-time, probably your second-largest college expense.

- **Computer and peripheral equipment** (e.g., printer, keyboard, mouse, etc.), software, and internet access used primarily for the beneficiary while enrolled. Software for sports, games, or hobbies is excluded, unless it's predominantly educational in nature.

- **Special needs services**, connected with enrollment or attendance by special needs students.

  Example: Sophia enrolls at a private college in a neighboring state, an eight-hour drive from her parents' home. Her tuition bill is $11,400 for her first year and her room and board in the on-campus dorms is $7,900. She buys a new laptop for school and a word processing software package for $1,050. Her mother uses her 529 to pay for all of these expenses.

One expense requires special attention: room and board. Don't go overboard when estimating how much you will spend! The "cost of attendance" covered in *Making a College Savings Plan* (Chapter 2) places an upper limit on how much you can withdraw to pay for room and board. If you spend more than the room and board estimate, then you will owe income tax and penalties on the excess.

> **Example:** During her junior year, Sophia rents a private room in an upscale apartment complex. Her total rent for the year is $12,400, significantly more than her college's estimate of $7,900 for room and board. Her father uses his 529 to pay all of her rent. During the next tax season, his accountant informs him that he owes federal income tax, state income tax, and a 10% penalty on the earnings portion of the $4,600 that exceeded the college's estimate.

In recent years, the 529 rules have been expanded to include the following expenses:

- **Trade school and registered apprenticeships**

- **K-12 tuition expenses, and**

- **Repayment of student loans.**

I cover these non-traditional uses for 529s in *Additional Ways to Use Your 529* (Chapter 9).

Finally, if your student has to withdraw from school after you've paid tuition using your 529, any refund becomes a non-qualifying expense. To find out how to handle tuition refunds, see *Tuition Refunds* (Chapter 10).

Non-Qualified Expenses

If an expense doesn't fit into one of the "qualified expense" categories, then you shouldn't use your 529 to pay for it. Non-qualified expenses include:

- **Application and testing fees**, including SAT, ACT, and Advanced Placement fees

- **Transportation expenses**, including airline tickets, gas money, auto insurance, or public transportation

- **Health insurance**

- **Extracurricular activity fees**

- **Personal expenses,** and

- **Room and board** for a student who is not enrolled at least half-time, or the portion that exceeds the cost of attendance estimate.

If you use your 529 to pay for a non-qualified expense, then you'll owe income tax and penalties on the earnings portion of your withdrawal. Learn more about penalties for excessive withdrawals in *Excessive Withdrawals* (Chapter 10).

Withdrawing Money from a 529 Account

There is no universal rule for how frequently you can withdraw money from your 529. However, individual plans may set limits. If you chose to, you could withdraw money as each expense happens, or you could group your expenses together into a single withdrawal.

You can choose any of the following recipients for your withdrawal:

1. **Pay the institution**. Depending on your plan, this could be as easy as specifying the university and your student's ID number. This method won't work for off-campus room and board or computer expenses.

2. **Pay the Account Owner.** Use this method if you paid for the expense yourself, either with your bank account, a credit card, loan proceeds, or some other way. Many plans can direct deposit money into your checking account.

3. **Pay the Beneficiary.** Use this method if your student paid the expense, whether from a bank account, credit card, student loan proceeds, or some other way. Your 529 plan will either send your student a check or direct deposit the money to their bank account.

Who you chose as recipient matters at tax time if you make any non-qualifying withdrawals:

- If the payee was either the educational institution or the beneficiary, then the **beneficiary** is responsible for any tax or penalties

- If the payee was the account owner, then the **account owner** is responsible for any tax or penalties.

Learn more about how to reduce your total tax bill by paying the beneficiary in *Reduce Your Total Tax Bill by Reimbursing the Student* (Chapter 10).

Eligible Educational Institutions

You can use your 529 at any school that qualifies for student aid programs offered by the U.S. Department of Education. Qualifying schools include most four-year universities and colleges throughout the United States, as well as two-year associate degree programs, trade schools, vocational schools, and most graduate and professional schools. Even international schools can qualify.

To see if your school qualifies, search for the school's Federal School Code at https://fafsa.ed.gov.

> **Example:** Fabian enrolls at Masarykova Univerzita in the Czech Republic. Because the school is eligible for U.S. federal student aid, Fabian's mother can use her 529 to pay for his expenses.

Withdrawal Deadlines

You must withdraw money from you 529 in the same year as the expense. Most savers will either pay the college directly when tuition is due or reimburse themselves as expenses occur. This approach is simplest and easy to understand.

Another option is to keep track of your expenses during the year and then make a single large withdrawal at the end of the year. The advantage of waiting until then is that your money has more time to compound. The disadvantage is that you'll have to wait to reimburse yourself, which may not work for your budget.

> **Example:** Fabian's spring semester tuition of $7,650 is due on January 1st. His mother, Claire, pays the tuition bill using her checking account instead of her 529. In December, Claire withdraws $7,650 from her 529, giving her an additional twelve months of tax-free growth. Assuming a 7% rate of return, her account grew an additional $553 by delaying the withdrawal.

Whatever approach you take, don't wait until the last day of December to make your withdrawal. Remember that plans are busy at the end of the year, and websites have a habit of crashing when it's inconvenient.

Lastly, if you pay a tuition bill in December, you must withdraw the money in December. It may make sense to wait to pay a tuition bill until January 1st to give yourself an additional year of tax-free growth.

Tax Forms to Watch for

Every year that you pay tuition or withdraw money from your 529, you'll receive the following tax forms:

1098-T

At the end of the year, your college will mail you Form 1098-T.[1] This form includes:

- The total tuition and related expenses paid to the school (box 1)

- Any scholarships or grants received from the institution (box 5), and

- Whether the student was at least half-time or not (box 8).

This form won't include room and board expenses, even if your student lived in on-campus housing. Your school might furnish you with a separate annual invoice that includes these expenses. You'll also use this form for various education-related tax credits and deductions (see *Scholarships, Grants and Tax Credits* (Chapter 6)).

1099-Q

If you withdrew money from your 529 during the year, the plan administrator will send you Form 1099-Q.[2] Both you and your student may receive separate copies of this form, depending on how you withdrew money from your account.

This form describes:

- The recipient of the withdrawals

- Total amount of withdrawals (box 1)

- How much of the withdrawal was considered earnings (box 2)

- How much of the withdrawal was considered contributions (box 3), and

- Information about rollovers and prepaid tuition plans.

Other Tax Forms

If you end up paying tax or penalties, you'll report the tax on Forms 1040 and 5329. You can learn more about these forms in *Tax Forms 1040 and 5329* (Chapter 10).

Record Keeping

Even though you'll receive official tax forms from your university, they won't list all of your qualified expenses, only tuition. You need to keep detailed records of your expenses to substantiate your withdrawals, in case of an audit. As long as you're following the rules and keeping records, you shouldn't be worried.

> **Example:** Claire used her 529 to pay for her son's college expenses. She instructed the plan to pay the university for tuition. Claire paid housing expenses using her own checking account. She keeps a spreadsheet that tracks her expenses throughout the year and reimburses herself from her 529 in December.
>
> In late January, Claire's son receives a 1098-T form for his tuition. Claire receives two separate 1099-Q forms from her 529 plan. The first lists her son as a recipient for the tuition paid directly to the university. The second lists Claire as the recipient, because she reimbursed herself for her son's housing expenses.

When Do I Need to Use All the Money in My 529 Account?

There is no federal rule on when a 529 must be depleted. Some plans set deadlines, but many plans have no deadline at all. You'll need to check with your plan for any deadline.

When you no longer need your 529 account to pay for college, you have several options:

- **Pay for graduate or professional school**. If your student is headed to law school, medical school, or any post-baccalaureate degree, you can use your 529 to pay for it.

- **Change the beneficiary to a sibling.** Or maybe to your spouse or yourself. Changing a beneficiary is covered in *Changing Beneficiaries* (Chapter 10).

- **Cash it out.** Be aware that you'll pay income tax and a 10% penalty on the earnings portion, and you may need to pay back any state tax break you received as well.

Summary

You're familiar with how to use your 529, including what expenses qualify and what to expect at tax time. For many families, being familiar with the first part of this book will be enough and they won't need to read further.

However, depending on your family's situation, there may be some unusual forks in your 529 journey. In the second part of this book, I'll walk you through some of these nuances and provide tips and strategies for maximizing your savings.

Here are some steps that you can take before you start Part 2.

Take Action!

Total Time: 25 to 30 minutes

1. Review the colleges or universities that your student plans on attending. Do they participate in the federal student financial aid programs? You can search for your school here: https://studentaid.gov/fafsa-app/FSCsearch

2. Make a plan for how you'll keep records when you start withdrawing from your 529. What method will you use: a spreadsheet, a notebook, a note on your phone, or some other method? You should keep printed versions of these records with the copies of your tax return.

3. Look up the details on your home state's 529 plan.

   a. Are there any special rules about how your home state treats non-qualifying distributions?

b. If your home state gives a tax break for contributing to a 529, what are its rules for reclaiming the tax break?

4. Without actually completing a distribution, check out how your 529 plan handles distributions. Does the plan support direct withdrawals to your bank account or your student's bank account? Does your plan have any deadlines for year-end distributions?

Eligible Expenses Record (Example)			
Date	**Amount**	**Category**	**Notes**
1/1/2021	-$793	Room & Board	Dorm and meal plan
1/4/2021	-$2,985	Tuition	Winter 2021, sophomore year
1/6/2021	-$462	Books & Supplies	Textbooks
2/1/2021	-$793	Room & Board	Dorm and meal plan
3/1/2021	-$793	Room & Board	Dorm and meal plan
4/1/2021	-$793	Room & Board	Dorm and meal plan
4/29/2021	-$724	Room & Board	Final dorm payment 🎉
8/1/2021	-$410	Room & Board	Off campus housing
8/23/2021	-$3,060	Tuition	Fall 2021, junior year
8/25/2021	-$342	Room & Board	Groceries
8/31/2021	-$552	Books & Supplies	Textbooks
		...	
12/1/2021	-$410	Room & Board	Off campus housing
12/14/2021	-$452	Room & Board	Groceries
12/16/2021	+$15,435	529 Withdrawal	Withdrawal for 2021 🐷

Balance   **$0**

---

[1] https://www.irs.gov/forms-pubs/about-form-1098-t

[2] https://www.irs.gov/forms-pubs/about-form-1099-q

Part 2

Uncommon Scenarios

Using a 529 to pay for college should be relatively simple: you open the account when your child is young, contribute to the account over the years, and then start withdrawing the money as the college expenses roll in, depleting it right as your student receives their diploma.

But life happens and complications arise. The rest of this book is dedicated to the "what if...?" aspects of 529s. You probably won't run into many of the topics in this section, because they're relatively uncommon. However, being aware of the exceptions can help you be prepared in case you do encounter them.

6

Scholarships, Grants, and Tax Credits

In recent years, approximately 86% of undergraduate students received some form of financial aid. A large portion of financial aid is through grants and scholarships. Additionally, the federal government offers tax credits and deductions for qualifying students and families, and sometimes employers help shoulder the expenses. Lastly, there are other tax-advantaged ways to save for college.

I'll categorize the "things that help make college more affordable" into two separate buckets: "college discounts," and "college savings." I'll briefly discuss how each bucket affects your 529.[1]

Bucket #1: College Discounts

There are several ways to reduce your college expenses, including scholarships, grants, tax credits, and employer-provided assistance.

Scholarships and Grants

Was your student awarded a scholarship or grant? Were they accepted into a prestigious, all-expense-paid military program? Is your student a dual citizen in a foreign country that provides a free college education to its citizens?

Congratulations on your good fortune! Way to go! It's every parent's dream to have their child receive a discount for their education.

No matter how good the scholarship or grant is, there's a good chance that it doesn't cover *every* eligible expense. Many scholarships only cover tuition. Even full scholarships that cover both tuition and room and board typically don't cover expenses such as books, supplies, equipment, or a computer.

> **Example:** Denzel's daughter earned a scholarship that covers both her tuition and her room and board expenses. However, it does not cover her books or

the purchase of a personal computer. Denzel uses his 529 to pay for these eligible expenses.

Please note that using a 529 to save for college could reduce your eligibility for need-based scholarships and grants. Learn more about how 529s impact financial aid in *529s and Financial Aid* (Chapter 7).

American Opportunity and Lifetime Learning Tax Credits

The American Opportunity Tax Credit (AOTC) and the Lifetime Learning Credit (LLC) are two federal income tax credits that help families with students. The AOTC and LLC can only be used for tuition, not room and board.

Eligibility for either of these credits depends on your income. For a taxpayer filing a joint return in 2021:

- The **American Opportunity Tax Credit** is reduced if your adjusted gross income (AGI) exceeds $160,000, and is completely phased out if your AGI exceeds $180,000.[2]

- The **Lifetime Learning Credit** is reduced if your AGI exceeds $118,000, and completely phased out if your AGI exceeds $138,000.[3]

Maximize the AOTC During Your Student's Senior Year

For most of their college years, your student will likely be listed as a dependent on your tax return. As a dependent, your student won't be able to claim the AOTC themselves. If your income is too high, your family will miss out on the credit altogether. In this case, is it possible to arrange it so that your student can claim the credit when you can't?

The answer is yes. Most academic years for colleges based in the United States end in the spring. If your student starts a full-time job following their spring graduation and then supports themselves for at least six months of the year, they cease to be your tax dependent and can then claim the AOTC for their final semester of school.

> **Example:** Ryan's salary disqualifies him for both the AOTC and LLC. His daughter, Michelle, is in her senior year of college. After graduating in May, Michelle lands a job in a neighboring state. Because she supports herself for more than half of the year and because her income is below the threshold, Michelle can take the full AOTC, saving her $2,500 in tax.

Employer-Provided Assistance

Many employers provide assistance in paying for higher education. The first $5,250 contributed by the employer is tax-free (in 2021). This benefit can be used to pay for tuition, fees, books, supplies, and equipment. It can't be used for room and board or transportation. Be aware that employer-provided assistance directly reduces your AOTC and LLC eligibility.

Bucket #2: College Savings

529s aren't the only tax-advantaged way to save for college. Other tax-advantaged ways to save include Coverdell ESAs, U.S. Savings Bonds, and IRAs. The general rule for this bucket is "no double dipping!" You can't use multiple saving methods to pay for the same expense.

I compare 529s with these additional savings methods in *Other Ways to Save for College* (Chapter 8).

Coverdell ESAs

Coverdell ESAs are a tax-advantaged way to save for college. Like a 529, you get tax-free growth and tax-free withdrawals. You can use both 529s and ESAs to pay for college expenses at the same time, but you can't use a 529 to pay for an expense that you also used your ESA to pay for, and vice versa.

U.S. Savings Bonds

When you use series EE and series I bonds issued by the U.S. government to pay for college, you may be able to exclude their interest on your income tax return.

Individual Retirement Accounts (IRAs)

Lastly, you can take an early distribution from your IRA to pay for qualified education expenses. You will owe regular income tax on the distribution, but the additional 10% penalty is waived.

The Buckets and Your 529

So, how do these two buckets affect your 529?

Everything in the "college discounts" bucket are exceptions to the 529 penalty. As long as your total withdrawals from the "college savings" bucket don't exceed your **total eligible expenses,** then you don't owe any penalty. If you withdraw more than that, then you will owe the penalty on the earnings portion of the excess. You may also end up paying back part of the state tax break.

> **Example:** Mark's total eligible expenses are $28,500 in 2022. His mother, Ashley, redeems Series I savings bonds worth $14,300 and withdraws an additional $14,200 from her 529. Mark earned a scholarship

worth $4,500 and Ashley was able to claim the full AOTC, or $2,500.

Ashley doesn't owe any penalty because her total withdrawals and redemptions equaled her total eligible expenses and because both the scholarship and AOTC are exceptions to the penalty.

Second, after subtracting everything in the "college discount" bucket from your total eligible expenses, you're left with your **net eligible expenses.** If your withdrawals from the "college savings" bucket exceed your net expenses, then you'll owe income tax on the earnings portion of the excess.

> **Example:** After subtracting the scholarship and the AOTC from his expenses, Mark's net eligible expenses are $21,500 in 2022. Because Ashley's total withdrawals and redemptions exceeded Mark's net eligible expenses by $7,000, Ashley will owe income tax on the earnings portion of her excessive withdrawal.

When Ashley receives her 1099-Q from her 529 plan, she learns that 56% of her excessive withdrawal was earnings. She'll owe both state and federal income tax on the earnings portion, or $3,920. She won't need to pay back any state income tax break, though, because her state has an exception for scholarships and the AOTC.

Other Ways to Pay for College

There are additional ways to save on college that you might run into on your journey that deserve mentioning: loans and work-study programs.

Loans and Work-Study Programs

Many families can't pay for college through working and saving their way to the finish line. Borrowing continues to be a popular way to pay for college. In 2021, new graduates had an estimated average student loan debt of $36,140.[4]

Borrowing isn't free money, however.[5] And even though both loans and work-study programs are considered financial aid, neither affects your ability to use your 529.

Whether you pay for college primarily through working and saving, through borrowing, or through a mixture of both, you should pass every expense through your 529 first to benefit from any state income tax break. I cover this strategy in more detail in *Which 529 Plan is Best for Me?* (Chapter 3).

Learn more about using 529s to pay off student loans in *Additional Ways to Use Your 529* (Chapter 9).

Summary

You can use your 529 whether your student earns a scholarship or grant, you qualify for education-related tax credits, or you're using other tax-advantaged ways to pay for eligible education expenses. In the next chapter, we'll dig more into how 529s affect financial aid.

Before you move on, here are some steps you can take:

Take Action!

Total Time: 10 minutes

1. Review your most recent tax return. How likely is it that you will qualify for either the AOTC or the LLC when your student enters college?

2. Will you be saving for college using a Coverdell ESA or savings bonds, in addition to a 529? Make a plan for how you'll use each savings method, including which one you'll spend down first. You can find more information in the next chapter, *529s and Financial Aid* (Chapter 7).

---

[1] If you want all of the gory details, check out IRS publication 970: https://www.irs.gov/forms-pubs/about-publication-970

[2] https://www.irs.gov/credits-deductions/individuals/aotc

[3] https://www.irs.gov/credits-deductions/individuals/llc

[4] https://educationdata.org/average-student-loan-debt-by-year

---

[5] I'm ignoring loan forgiveness programs

7

529s and Financial Aid

During the 2020-2021 academic year, most families received some form of financial aid:

- 56% of families received scholarships

- 50% of families received grants, and

- 47% of families received loans, including both subsidized and unsubsidized.[1]

The subject of student financial aid deserves its own book. This chapter details how your 529 could impact your financial aid prospects.

To keep it simple, I'll focus on the Free Application for Federal Student Aid (FAFSA), used by most schools to calculate a student's financial aid "need." I touch briefly on the other financial aid calculator, the proprietary College Scholarship Service Profile (CSS Profile), later in this chapter.

Note: Congress passed the FAFSA Simplification Act in December 2020, which will change the FAFSA significantly over the next few years. The following should be accurate enough for the 2022-2023 aid year.

Your Financial Aid Need

All need-based financial aid calculations start with the "cost of attendance" (COA) that you learned about in *What Is the Advertised Price of College?* (Chapter 2). The COA is the total cost that your university expects a new freshman to incur during their first year of college. The COA includes not just tuition and fees, but also books, supplies, room & board, transportation, and personal expenses.

Your financial aid eligibility depends on your "expected family contribution," or EFC. The EFC quantifies how much you and your student should be expected to contribute to your student's education expenses.

You don't need to calculate your EFC yourself.[2] There are many online calculators that can help you estimate your

EFC.[3] The calculators ask questions about you and your student's income and savings to determine your EFC.

Once you have your COA and EFC estimate, you can calculate your student's financial aid need, like this:

Financial Aid Need = COA - EFC

If your need is more than zero, then your student is eligible for some form of student aid.

It may surprise you to learn that neither your income from this year or your income from last year affects the FAFSA. Instead, the FAFSA looks at your tax return from two years ago, sometimes called the "prior-prior year." For example, if you are filling out the 2022-2023 FAFSA, you'll be asked for information about your 2020 tax return.

529 Account Ownership and Financial Aid

Under the current rules, who owns the 529 can impact your EFC. The typical scenario is a 529 owned by a parent. But the owner could be a grandparent, the student, or someone else.[4]

Here are some of the ways 529 ownership impacts financial aid calculations:

- **A dependent student with a 529 owned by either the parent or student:** the 529 reduces financial aid as much as 5.64%.[5] If your 529 balance was $10,000 when filling out the FAFSA, your financial aid could drop as much as $564.

- **An independent student with no dependents other than a spouse with a 529 owned by the student:** the 529 reduces financial aid by a 20% factor. If the 529 balance was $10,000, aid would be reduced by as much as $2,000.

- **An independent student with dependent(s) other than a spouse with a 529 owned by the student:** the 529 reduces financial aid by as much as 3.29%. If the 529 balance was $10,000, financial aid could be reduced by as much as $329.

- **All other cases (e.g., grandparent-owner, etc.):** the account is not considered an asset of the student. Prior to 2022, withdrawals from these 529s counted as untaxed income and reduces financial aid by as much as 50%. In 2022 and beyond, the updated FAFSA rules exclude these accounts altogether from the EFC calculations.

Use Parent- and Student-Owned 529s First

To optimize your financial aid eligibility, use any parent- and student-owned 529s before you use 529s owned by a grandparent or other family member. Doing this means the parent- and student-owned accounts won't count against you in future years.

Example: Zane's 529 has a balance of $26,780. The first time his daughter fills out the FAFSA, the 529 reduces financial aid by $1,510. Zane doesn't use his 529 to pay expenses during freshman year, allowing the account to grow to $28,922. When he fills out the parental questionnaire on the FAFSA for his daughter's sophomore year, Zane is dismayed to find that his 529 reduced their aid again, this time by $1,631. He immediately starts using his 529, increasing financial aid eligibility in subsequent years.

Maximize Your Tax-Advantaged Retirement Accounts

This chapter focuses on how your 529 impacts your student aid. But it's worth mentioning that contributing to your tax-advantaged retirement accounts (e.g., 401(k)s, 403(b)s, IRAs, etc.) will increase your eligibility for financial aid because they aren't included in the FAFSA calculations. If you're choosing between contributing to your IRA and contributing to your 529, you should know that doing the former will improve your financial aid prospects.

529s and the College Scholarship Service Profile

Some schools use the proprietary College Scholarship Service Profile (CSS Profile) from the College Board to determine financial aid eligibility. It has a longer set of questions than the FAFSA and measures some assets differently.

Here are the main differences:

- All 529 plans that list the student as beneficiary are considered by the CSS. Meanwhile, the FAFSA only considers accounts owned by the student or their parents.

- On the CSS Profile, 529 plans owned by the parent reduce aid by 5%. On the FAFSA, this reduction in aid can be as high as 5.64%.

- On the CSS Profile, 529 plans owned by a dependent student reduce aid by 25%. On the FAFSA, 529s owned by students are treated as parental assets, reducing aid by as much as 5.64%, and 529s owned by independent students reduce aid by as much as 20%.

Describing all the ways that the CSS Profile differs from the FAFSA is beyond the scope of this book.[6]

Summary

When held by a parent or student, 529 accounts impact your financial aid no more than does a savings, checking, or brokerage account. In the next chapter, I'll touch on these other ways that you can save for college and show you how they compare with using a 529. Before you read on, here are some actions you can take:

Take Action!

Total Time: 20 to 30 minutes

1. Calculate your Expected Family Contribution, or EFC. Search online for "efc calculator" or "fafsa worksheet". At minimum, you'll need the following:

   a. Your latest tax return

   b. Amounts that you contributed to your tax-deferred retirement accounts

   c. Current balances of savings, checking, brokerage accounts, etc.

2. Subtract your EFC from your COA that you calculated in *Making a College Savings Plan* (Chapter 2). How much need-based aid would you qualify for today?

3. Is your student the beneficiary of 529s owned by a grandparent or another relative? What is your plan for how to use those 529s?

4. Does your student qualify for a Roth IRA?[7] If so, consider maximizing their Roth contribution to increase your financial aid eligibility.

---

[1] https://www.salliemae.com/about/leading-research/how-america-pays-for-college/

[2] If you want the detailed FAFSA formulas, you can find them here: https://fsapartners.ed.gov/sites/default/files/attachments/2020-08/2122EFCFormulaGuide.pdf

[3] Example: https://studentaid.gov/aid-estimator/

[4] Learn more about student account owners in Chapter 10: *Student Account Owners*

[5] The FAFSA process first multiplies parental assets by 12%, and then by another 47% after grouping parental assets with income. However, 5.64% is a worst-case scenario, and families with less income and assets may have their 529 reduce their financial aid even less.

[6] See https://blog.collegeboard.org/whats-difference-between-css-profile-and-fafsa

[7] To contribute to an IRA, an individual must have earned income

8

Other Ways to Save for College

A 529 isn't the only way to save for college. In this chapter, I'll cover other ways you can save for college.

Banking Accounts

Bank accounts are perhaps the most obvious way to save. As of 2019, nearly 95% of U.S. households have either a checking or savings account at a bank or credit union.[1] Chances are good that you already have either a savings or a checking account.

Besides simplicity, bank accounts offer another advantage: there are no rules on how you spend the money. You don't have to worry about whether something is a qualified education expense or not. Many other saving methods share this advantage, including CDs, brokerage accounts, and savings bonds.

As convenient as they can be, bank accounts aren't great for college savings. When compared with a 529, disadvantages include:

- **Negative rate of return, after inflation.** In 2021, the national average interest rate for savings accounts was 0.06%. If you had $10,000 of savings in 2004, just 8 years later your account balance would only be $10,109.[2] Inflation over that same period averaged 2.18%, sinking your purchasing power to $6,825.[3]

- Not only does inflation eat away at your savings, but so too can federal and state income taxes. Interest from bank accounts is **taxed as ordinary income**. Assuming an average marginal tax rate of 22%, you kept $85 of the $109.

- Lastly, because you can withdraw the money at any time, **it takes discipline to not dip into your college savings.** This is true whether you're using your everyday spending account to save or whether you're using a separate account.

  Example: Claire opened a savings account to pay for her son's college. She's been depositing $100 each month for fifteen years at an average annual interest rate of 0.5%. Her marginal tax rate is 22% and she's been paying tax each year on the interest. Claire has contributed a total of $18,000 (15 years * 12 months * $100) and she has paid $154 in tax. Her final account balance is $18,534.[4] During this same period, inflation averaged 2% per year, giving her a negative rate of return of -1.61%.[5]

Certificate of Deposit (CDs)

Putting your college savings in CDs has one advantage over traditional bank accounts: **reduced temptation** because of early termination fees, usually a few months of interest.

Compared with 529s, CDs have the same disadvantages as regular bank accounts do:

- **Low interest rates.** In early 2022, you could find 1- or 2-year CDs that had 0.8% interest rates, putting them marginally ahead of some high-yield savings accounts. Just like a savings account, inflation turns it into a negative rate of return.

- Like your savings account, any earnings are **taxed as ordinary income** by both federal and state governments.

  Example: Over a ten-year period, Claire invested $2,000 in 5-year CDs, each year. The CDs have an average interest rate of 1.0%. Her total contribution of $20,000 is now worth $20,717.[6] Claire paid $208 in federal income tax.[7] Inflation over the same period was 2%, giving Claire a negative rate of return of -1.22%.[8]

Brokerage Accounts

While not as common as checking or savings accounts, about one-third of U.S. households have a taxable brokerage account, making these another popular way to save for college.[9] Brokerage accounts have several advantages over traditional banking accounts and CDs, including:

- Significantly **better rates of return** due to a wider range of investment options, that include stocks, bonds, ETFs, commodities, etc.

- Your earnings are **taxed at a lower rate** than a regular bank account, assuming you hold shares longer than a year. With tax-loss harvesting strategies, you could boost your savings even more.

- The **additional friction of selling** investments can reduce the temptation to dip into your savings.

Compared with 529s, there are still some major downsides when using a brokerage account to save for college, including:

- Although it's at a lower rate, federal and state governments **tax your earnings**. When you sell appreciated assets to pay for college, you might simultaneously face a large tax bill.

- You are choosing between a potentially **overwhelming number of investment options**.

  Example: Over the past fifteen years, Claire has saved for her son's college expenses by making periodic purchases in an index fund that had an annual average return of 8%. She's contributed a total of $18,000 over the years and her investments are now worth $32,583.[10] When Claire sells the shares to pay for college, she realizes a capital gains tax bill of $2,187, leaving $30,395 for college expenses.

Brokerage accounts have some advantages over 529s:

- Withdrawing money from your 529 when your student received a scholarship means paying **regular income tax on the earnings**, which is probably more than your capital gains tax rate.

- If your student doesn't use the 529, you'll end up paying an additional 10% on your withdrawal, which combined with your regular income tax rate makes this significantly higher than paying capital gains tax.

Using a brokerage account, you can usually replicate the investment options in a 529 and usually for lower fees. You may be better off skipping the 529 and saving for college using a brokerage account if any of the following are true:

- You don't receive a state tax break for 529 contributions, and

- You feel there's a significant chance your student won't attend college or trade school. If you have multiple children, it's a smaller risk that none of them will use your 529 savings.

UTMA/UGMA Accounts

The Universal Transfer to Minors and Universal Gift to Minors Acts (UTMA and UGMA, respectively) made it easier for parents to save and invest on behalf of their child. These accounts generally share the same advantages and disadvantages as regular brokerage accounts.

An additional advantage of UTMA and UGMA accounts is that the first $1,050 of earnings are usually tax free if the child is under the age of 19. And the next $1,050 is taxed at the child's rate, which is usually lower than the parents' tax rate.

One major downside of UTMAs and UGMAs that isn't shared with 529s is that **the beneficiary gains control** of the account when they come of age. The age varies between states but is often at 18 years (UGMA) or 21 (UTMA). It's possible that your child will be tempted to use the money for something other than college.

> **Example:** Claire lives in Alabama and opens a UTMA for her son, Fabian, when he is born. When he turns 19 (the age of majority in Alabama), control of the account switches to Fabian. Luckily, Fabian is a driven child and spends the balance *mostly* on education, with an occasional splurge here and there on non-education expenses.

Savings Bonds

The EE- and I-series savings bonds issued by the U.S. government are popular ways to save. When compared with a savings or checking account, advantages include:

- **Reduced temptation.** You can't cash the bonds in the first year and you lose three months of interest if you cash them out in the first five years.

- You can **exclude the interest on your federal income tax return** if you cash them out during the same year you paid higher education expenses. To qualify, your modified adjusted gross income (MAGI) must be below $98,200 in 2021 ($154,800 for joint returns), with a partial exclusion if your income is between $83,200 and

$98,200 (between $124,800 and $154,800 for joint returns).

- The interest on savings bonds is **excluded from state income tax**.

Using savings bonds for education is reported on Form 8815.[11]

> **Example:** Claire purchased series I savings bonds over many years. When her son starts college, Claire cashes out some of the bonds to pay his $14,204 tuition bill. The bonds she sold had earned $3,679 of interest. Her MAGI is $87,000, giving her a partial deduction of $2,747 bond interest. Claire pays federal income tax on the remaining $932 of interest.

Savings bonds come with significant downsides when compared with a 529:

- **Low interest rates.** Series EE bonds pay 0.10% interest (early 2022[12]), worse than many high-yield savings accounts. Rates for Series I bonds are higher because the rate includes an inflation component. As of early 2022, series I bonds had rates as high as 7.12%.[13]

- **Limits on how many you can buy.** You can buy $10,000 of series EE bonds and $10,000 of series I bonds each year. Using your tax return, you can purchase an additional $5,000 of series I bonds. 529s have contribution limits that are 10 to 20 times larger.

- Savings bonds can **be only used for tuition and fees,** not room and board or computer equipment.[14]

Retirement Accounts

Faced with high education expenses and little savings, it can be tempting to use your workplace retirement account to bridge the gap. Usually this means either borrowing against your retirement account or making a hardship withdrawal.

Borrowing Against Your 401(k)

Some workplace retirement plans (e.g., 401(k), 403(b), and 457(b)) may allow participants to borrow against their vested balance. Other accounts, such as IRAs, don't allow this option. If you choose to borrow against your retirement plan, here are some things to consider:

- Your loan is **limited to either 50% of your vested balance or $50,000,** whichever is less.

- You generally have **five years to pay back any loan.** Otherwise it turns into a withdrawal and you'll owe both tax and penalties.

- **If you leave your company**, you may be immediately required to pay back the loan balance.

- If you break the rules, your loan turns into a disqualified distribution and **you will owe both income tax and penalties** on the withdrawal.

- Unlike a hardship withdrawal, **a loan doesn't count as income and won't affect your application for need-based financial aid,** as long as the loan proceeds aren't sitting in your bank account when you fill out the FAFSA application.

- While the money isn't in your retirement plan, you're **missing out on future compounding.**

  Example: Claire borrows from her 401(k) plan to pay her son's tuition bill. Claire's vested balance is $52,356, enabling her to borrow $26,178. The 401(k) provider charges her a $100 fee to set up the loan. The interest rate is 7%, giving her a $520 monthly payment to ensure the loan is paid back in five years. Claire suspends her contributions during the five years, forfeiting her employer's matching contribution.

Hardship Withdrawals from Your 401(k)

It may be tempting to use your workplace retirement accounts to pay for college before you reach retirement age,[15] but doing so has some significant disadvantages, including:

- First, **your plan must allow it.** Most plans limit your ability to withdraw funds while you're employed, although paying tuition may count as a "hardship" withdrawal.

- Even if you're able to withdraw money, you'll be taxed on your withdrawal at your **ordinary income tax rate.** It's likely you're in your peak earning years, so expect a big tax bill.

- If you're younger than 59½, you'll have to pay an **additional 10% penalty.**

- If you're desperate enough to withdraw money from your retirement account to pay for school, you probably qualify for need-based financial aid. However, withdrawing money from a retirement account counts as income, **making you less eligible for need-based aid.** Timing withdrawals in the student's junior or senior years could alleviate this.

- Generally you can't do a hardship withdrawal until you've exhausted your ability to borrow from your retirement plan (see *Borrowing Against Your 401(k)*, Chapter 8).

- Many plans **prohibit contributing to the plan for six months** following a withdrawal. If your workplace retirement plan has an employer match, you may forfeit it by not contributing.

Remember, you can get loans to pay for school, but no one will lend you money to retire.

> **Example:** Claire withdraws $12,900 as a hardship withdrawal to pay for fall tuition. When tax season rolls around, she owes an additional $4,386[16] on her federal taxes and an additional $472 in state income tax.[17] She'll also need to report the withdrawal on a future FAFSA, negatively impacting their financial aid eligibility.

Roth IRA

The Roth IRA rules have an exception for withdrawals for education expenses. Things to consider:

- **You can always withdraw your contributions** from your Roth IRA without paying income tax or penalties on the withdrawal.

- Withdrawing money from your Roth IRA **forfeits years of compounding.** On the other hand, choosing to contribute to a 529 instead of a Roth IRA is really no different.

- If you're older than 59½, you can withdraw earnings without paying either income tax or a penalty. If you're younger than 59½, you'll pay income tax if you withdraw any earnings. The 10% early withdrawal penalty is waived if you use the money for qualified education expenses, which include: tuition, fees, books, supplies, and room and board for students that are at least half-time.

- Buying **a computer** for school using your Roth IRA **is not a qualified expense.**

- Using your Roth IRA to pay for education expenses could **increase the total amount of income tax** you'll pay over your lifetime.

- Retirement accounts (including Roth IRAs) aren't included by the FAFSA. Keeping the money in your retirement account will increase your financial aid prospects, compared to a 529.

  Example: When Denzel's daughter heads off to college, he taps into the contribution portion of his Roth IRA to pay the tuition bill. He doesn't owe any federal income tax, but forfeits years of compounding toward his retirement goal.

  Example: Sophia is a freshman. She opened a Roth IRA when she started working at the local pool at age fifteen. She's contributed $10,000 over the past three years and the account has grown to $11,902. When she enters college, she completely cashes out the account, foregoing decades of compounding. She's in the 10% tax bracket and will pay $190 of income tax on the $1,902 of gain. Because she's using the money for eligible education expenses, Sophia doesn't owe the 10% early-withdrawal penalty.

If you use both a 529 and a Roth IRA to fund college, make sure your total withdrawals from both don't exceed your total eligible expenses. If they do, you'll end up owing a 10% penalty on the earnings portion of the excess withdrawal.

Coverdell Education Savings Account

Like 529s, Coverdell Education Savings Accounts (ESA)[18] were designed for college savings. Like a 529, you contribute to an ESA using after-tax money. ESAs receive tax-free growth and tax-free withdrawals. And like a 529, you're penalized if you use your ESA for non-qualified expenses.

What does a Coverdell ESA offer that a 529 doesn't?

- ESAs have **more investment options,** allowing you to invest in individual stocks, bonds, mutual funds, ETFs, etc.

- ESAs have **no spending limits on eligible K-12 expenses**. However, even though ESAs don't have an upper limit, annual contribution limits (see below) reduce this advantage.

- You can open ESAs at many **popular banks and brokerage firms.** Options for opening a 529 are more limited.

Coverdell ESAs have significant limitations:

- **Age limits.** No contributions are allowed after the beneficiary turns 18.

- **Funds must be used before the beneficiary turns 30.** You can roll over your ESA into a 529 if you run up into this deadline.

- **$2,000 annual contribution limit, per beneficiary,** not per account. You'll need to coordinate with any relatives who also open a Coverdell ESA for your student in order to keep the total contribution below $2,000. 529s don't have annual contribution limits.

- **Income limits.** You can't contribute to an ESA if your modified adjusted gross income (MAGI) is more than $110,000 ($200,000 for joint returns).[19]

- Coverdell ESAs often come with **higher fees and expenses.**

- Unlike 529s, there are usually **no state tax breaks** for contributing to an ESA.

  Example: Nicole opened an ESA for her son when he was born in 2004. She contributed $2,000 for each of the first fourteen years, but for the last four years her income was too high. She invested in individual stocks with mixed success, averaging an annual return of 5%. When her son begins school in 2022, Nicole's account will have grown to $47,645.[20] As long as she uses it for qualified expenses, she'll pay no tax on the nearly $20k of gain.

Collectibles, Real Estate, etc.

Perhaps you're considering paying for college using a Beanie Baby[21] or Pokémon collection. Or, maybe it's with Bitcoin or rental income from a duplex that you bought years ago. These options are all suboptimal for college savings because they don't have tax-free growth, have higher maintenance costs, and receive no state tax breaks.

Summary

The primary benefits that set 529s apart are tax-free growth, tax-free withdrawals, and state income tax breaks. Their downsides include penalties on non-eligible expenses and a narrow set of investment options.

Take Action!

Total Time: 20 minutes

1. Make a list of your accounts, including checking, savings, brokerage, Roth IRAs, etc. How will these accounts fit into your college expense plan?

2. If you plan on borrowing from your workplace retirement account to pay for college, ask yourself the following questions:

   a. Does your workplace retirement plan allow loans? Not all plans do.

   b. How much have you vested? Remember that you can only borrow up to 50% of the vested amount or $50,000, whichever is lower.

   c. What are the fees for borrowing from your 401k? What is the interest rate and what will your monthly payment be?

   d. Does your company match your contributions and will you continue contributing to get the match during your loan period?

   e. Have you exhausted all other options before you dip into your retirement savings?

3. If you're planning on using savings bonds or a Coverdell ESA for college expenses, review the income limits to

make sure your modified adjusted gross income (MAGI) doesn't exceed them.[22]

---

[1] https://www.fdic.gov/analysis/household-survey/index.html

[2] Excel forumla: =fv((0.06%)/12, (2022-2004)*12, 0, -10000)

[3] See https://fred.stlouisfed.org/series/T20YIEM. Excel formula =fv((0.06%-2.18%)/12, (2022-2004)*12, 0, -10000)

[4] Excel formula: =fv((0.5%/12)*(1-22%), 12*15, -100, 0)

[5] .5% interest * (1 - 22% tax rate) - 2% inflation

[6] Excel formula: =fv(((1%)*(1-22%)),10,2000,0)

[7] Excel formula: =fv(((1%)),10,2000,0) - fv(((1%)*(1-22%)),10,2000,0)

[8] 1% interest rate * (1 - 22% tax rate) - 2% inflation

[9] https://www.finrafoundation.org/sites/finrafoundation/files/A-Snapshot-of-Investor-Households-in-America_0_0_0.pdf

[10] Excel formula: =fv(8%,15,18000/15,0)

[11] https://www.irs.gov/forms-pubs/about-form-8815

[12] https://www.treasurydirect.gov/indiv/products/prod_eebonds_glance.htm

[13] https://www.treasurydirect.gov/indiv/products/prod_ibonds_glance.htm

[14] See IRS Publication 970 for more details: https://www.irs.gov/pub/irs-pdf/p970.pdf

[15] For tax-advantaged retirement accounts, retirement age is generally 59½

16 Assuming a federal marginal tax rate of 24%, she owes $2,096 in regular income tax and a $1,290 penalty (10%)

17 Assuming a state income state tax of 3.65%

18 Since they are defined in section 530 of the US Code of Laws, it's a wonder that they aren't called 530 plans.

19 This is the 2022 limit. You can make a partial contribution if your MAGI is between $95,000 and $110,000 ($190,000 to $220,000 for joint returns).

20 Excel formula: =fv(5%,4,0,fv(5%,14,2000))

21 Okay, paying for college using Beanie Babies is likely exceedingly rare!

22 IRS Publication 970 covers tax benefits for education: https://www.irs.gov/pub/irs-pdf/p970.pdf

9

Additional Ways to Use Your 529

When 529s were created in 1996, they were intended for college savings. Their use was expanded in 2017 to include tuition for elementary and secondary school (K-12). The rules were expanded again in 2019 to include trade school and registered apprenticeship programs, and repayment of student loans.[1]

Even though the federal government expanded the use of 529s, not all states have adopted the changes. Your state may levy income tax and/or penalties for any use other than for higher education. Before you use your account in these non-traditional ways, check with your home state's 529 rules.

> **Example:** Tyson lives in California. He started 529s for his two sons when they were born. His original plan was to use the 529s to pay for college, but now he's decided he wants to use them to pay tuition at a private Catholic school. As of 2022, California has not accepted the expanded use of 529s for K-12 expenses and Tyson will need to pay both state income tax and an additional 2.5% penalty tax if he uses his 529s in this way.

K-12 Tuition Expenses

The use of 529 funds for K-12 tuition is limited to $10,000 per year, per beneficiary. The elementary or secondary school can be public, private, or religious. Daycare or preschool expenses are not eligible expenses.

Trade School and Registered Apprenticeships

Not all children are college-bound. In 2019, Congress expanded 529 rules to include trade schools and registered apprenticeships as eligible institutions. The eligible expenses for trade school and registered apprenticeships are the same as they are for traditional four-year universities and community colleges, including:

- Tuition and mandatory fees

- Textbooks, mandatory supplies, and equipment

- Computers, internet access, and peripherals

- Room and board (if enrolled at least half-time and for expenses incurred during the academic period), and

- Special needs expenses.

A rule of thumb for whether your 529 can be used at a particular trade school or not is whether you can use federal student aid to pay for tuition there. If you can, then you can use your 529. To see if a trade school qualifies, search for the school using the Federal School Code Search at studentaid.gov.[2]

> **Example:** Camille's son wants to attend Jenny Lea Academy of Cosmetology in Johnson City, Tennessee. Camille finds the school's Federal School Code, #016051, by searching at StudentAid.gov.[3] She can use her 529 to pay for her son's eligible education expenses.

Apprenticeship programs must be registered and certified by the Secretary of Labor to qualify.

Student Loan Repayment

Another recent rule change allows 529s to be used to pay off as much as $10,000 of student loans. This is a lifetime limit per beneficiary. You can also use your 529 to pay off student loan debt for a sibling of a beneficiary.

One of the reasons you would use a 529 to save for school is to avoid debt. Taking a student loan when you still have money remaining in your 529 is probably not the greatest idea. However, using a 529 might make sense if:

- You pass loan payments through a 529 for the state tax break, or[4]

- You have money left over in a sibling's 529.

  Example: Sophia is a resident of Virginia and recently finished a graduate degree, racking up some student loan debt. Her student loan debt payment is $467/month. She opens a 529 account and passes each payment through the account. Over the next 22 months, her contributions have saved her $575 in state income tax.

Qualifying loans must have been used solely to pay for qualified higher education expenses incurred by you, your spouse, or one of your dependents while the loan recipient was an eligible student.[5] Loans that qualify are federal direct loans (either subsidized or unsubsidized), PLUS

Loans, and direct consolidated loans. You can't use your 529 to pay off a personal loan made by either you or a relative to the student.

If your student is offered a loan but they don't need it, you may consider taking the loan, funding a 529 with it, then paying off the loan immediately. This strategy can boost your student's credit score, but is hampered by the loan origination fee (1.057% of the loan balance, in 2022), interest payments, and the $10,000 lifetime limit.

> **Example:** Jill is a resident of Virginia and is awarded an unsubsidized student loan of $5,500. The loan comes with an origination fee of $58 and an interest rate of 3.73%. She deposits the proceeds into a 529 account, saving $316 in state income tax.[6] After six months, she pays off the loan balance of $5,662, a net gain of $154.[7]

If you use a 529 to pay down a student loan, you can't take the student loan interest deduction at the same time. Remember, no double dipping!

Take Action!

Total Time: 20 minutes

1. Familiarize yourself with your home state's 529 rules for non-traditional use.

a. Does your home state levy income tax or additional penalties?

b. Does your home state "clawback" any tax breaks?

---

[1] Through the Tax Cuts and Jobs (TCJA) Act (2017) and the Setting Every Community Up for Retirement Enhancement (SECURE) Act (2019)

[2] Through the Tax Cuts and Jobs (TCJA) Act (2017) and the Setting Every Community Up for Retirement Enhancement (SECURE) Act (2019)

[3] https://studentaid.gov/fafsa-app/FSCsearch/ compare;direction=next;from=list;schoolCode=016051

[4] Subject to your home state's tax break rules

[5] https://uscode.house.gov/view.xhtml? req=(title:26%20section:221%20edition:prelim), section (221)(d)(1)

[6] $5,500 * 5.75%

[7] Excel formula: =fv(3.73%/12, 6, 0, -5500 - 58)

10

Uncommon Scenarios

Although you may never encounter the scenarios in this chapter, being aware of them could save you from future headaches. Many of the scenarios come with tax consequences and I recommend that you seek the advice of a qualified tax advisor before attempting any of them.

Excessive Withdrawals

Many savers won't have the problem of withdrawing too much from their 529, but it's helpful to understand the consequences in case it happens to you. Why would you withdraw too much? Possible scenarios include:

- You saved more than you needed to cover your education expenses. This could happen if your student received a scholarship or other financial aid or if you qualified for a tax credit.

- Your student had to withdraw from school and you received a tuition refund.

- Your room and board expenses exceeded the college's cost of attendance estimate.

- You withdrew to pay for non-qualified expenses, such as travel or personal expenses.

- You used both a 529 and another tax-advantaged way to pay for the same expense.

If you withdrew too much, you'll owe:

- Federal income tax

- An additional 10% penalty

- State income tax from your home state (if applicable), and maybe additional state penalties, and

- Your home state may require you to pay back any tax break you received from your original contributions.

Any federal income tax, state income tax, and the 10% penalty only apply to the **earnings** portion of your non-qualified withdrawal, **not your original contributions** or

basis. Unlike a Roth IRA, you can't withdraw the contribution portion by itself. Instead, withdrawals will always be part contributions and part earnings.

> **Example:** Ashley withdraws a total of $8,136 from her 529 account in 2022. Her 1099-Q statement from her 529 plan attributes $5,468 as contribution (67.2%) and $2,668 as earnings (32.8%). While doing her federal income tax return, she realizes that $2,000 of her withdrawals were non-qualified expenses. So $656 of the earnings portion ($2,000 * 32.8%) will be subject to both federal income tax, the 10% penalty, and state income tax.

Exceptions to the 10% Penalty

You won't owe the 10% penalty if any of the following apply:

- Your student received a tax-free scholarship or grant, or other non-taxable education assistance (excluding gifts or inheritances)

- Your student received veteran's educational assistance

- Your student received employer-provided educational assistance

- Your student attended a designated U.S. military academy

- You qualified for the American opportunity or lifetime learning credits, or

- Your beneficiary dies or is designated disabled.

You will still owe income tax. In these scenarios, your 529 behaves like a tax-deferred savings account.

> **Example:** Nicole's total education expenses during 2022 were $25,678. Her son earned a scholarship of $5,700. Nicole also qualified for a full AOTC credit: $2,500. After subtracting the scholarship and the credit, Nicole's net qualified education expenses are $17,478.
>
> Nicole withdrew $25,000 from her 529 during 2022. Because she withdrew less than her total education expenses ($25,678), she doesn't owe the 10% penalty. Because she withdrew more than her net qualified education expenses ($17,478), she does owe income tax on the earnings portion of her withdrawal that exceeded her net expenses ($7,522).
>
> When Nicole receives her 1099-Q from her 529 plan, she discovers that 36.4% of her withdrawal was earnings, or $2,738. Nicole is in the 22% marginal tax bracket and owes $602 on her 2022 federal income tax return. Nicole's home state is New Hampshire, which has no state income tax.

Reduce Your Total Tax Bill by Reimbursing the Student

It's likely that your student is in a lower tax bracket than you are. You can take advantage of this difference by reimbursing your student for expenses instead of yourself. This strategy only matters if some of your withdrawal is taxable, which could happen if your student receives a scholarship or if you qualify for a tax credit.

> **Example:** Continuing from the previous example, Nicole directs her 529 to pay the university for her son's tuition bill of $8,500. She reimburses her son for $12,000 of living expenses, and she reimburses herself for the remaining $4,500.
>
> At tax time, both Nicole and her son receive separate 1099-Qs from her 529 plan. When filing their income tax returns, Nicole and her son allocate all of the excessive withdrawal to her son's tax return, or $7,522. Because he is in the 10% tax bracket, he owes $274 of tax on the earnings portion ($2,738 of earnings * 10%), saving them together $328 in federal income tax.

Tuition Refunds

Life happens and a student may need to withdraw from school. If you withdrew funds for eligible education expenses but are now expecting a refund, your withdrawal just became disqualified and subject to both income tax and the 10% penalty, in addition to any tax and penalties from your home state.

You can avoid paying the tax and penalties by re-contributing the refunded money back into your 529 within 60 days.

> **Example:** Nicole's son falls ill during his first semester and withdraws. His university refunds $4,487 of his tuition. Because Nicole used 529 funds to pay tuition, she re-contributes the refund back into the 529. She avoids paying federal and state income tax and the 10% penalty on the earnings.

Coordinating Withdrawals with ESAs and Savings Bonds

You can pay for college expenses using a mix of 529s, Coverdell ESAs, and savings bonds. Keep your total withdrawals below your total eligible expenses to avoid taxes and penalties. If you withdraw more than your total eligible expenses, you will owe both income tax and a 10% penalty on the excess. You should also coordinate with any family member, such as a grandparent, who may have a 529 or ESA with your student as beneficiary.

Tax Forms 1040 and 5329

If you only made qualified withdrawals, you won't need to do anything when you file your federal income tax return. However, if you paid for non-qualified expenses using your 529 account, these withdrawals will show up a couple different ways when you file your income tax return.

First, the earnings portion of the non-qualifying withdrawals is included in your taxable income on Form 1040 Schedule 1, line 8z (for tax year 2021).

If you made non-qualifying withdrawals that were subject to the penalty (review the exceptions earlier in this chapter), then you'll file Form 5329, *Additional Taxes on Qualified Plans (Including IRAs) and Other Tax-Favored Accounts*. In 2021, the section that applied to 529s was Part II. After calculating the penalty on Form 5329, you'll report the penalty on Form 1040, Schedule 2, line 8 (for tax year 2021).

> **Example:** During 2021, Elise made $3,514 in non-qualifying withdrawals, of which 45% was earnings, or $1,581. Her grandson received a scholarship for $1,220.
>
> When she filed her 2021 income tax return, Elise reported $1,581 of extra income on her Form 1040, Schedule 1, line 8z. Because she is in the 32%

marginal tax bracket, Elise's income tax increases by $506. The amount of her withdrawal that is subject to the 10% penalty is 45% earnings * ($3,514 withdrawal - $1,220 scholarship), or $1,032. Her penalty is $103, which she reports using Form 5329 and on Form 1040, Schedule 2, line 8.

Don't Worry Too Much About Taxes or Penalties

If worries about taxes and penalties prevent you from opening a 529, then here are some thoughts to put your mind at ease:

- **Income tax and the 10% penalty only apply to earnings.** Your contributions were already taxed and are safe from any additional income tax or penalty.

- **You received tax-free compounding.** The 10% penalty can be annoying, but don't forget that your 529 received tax-free compounding, unlike a regular taxable brokerage account.

- If you **choose your student as the recipient,** together with your student you may end up paying zero additional income tax, depending on your student's marginal tax bracket.

- **Even if your state recaptures the state tax break, you are no worse off.** Putting on your rose-colored glasses, you could see this as an interest-free loan from your state.

Maximize your 529 account by only using it for qualified expenses. But don't let the fear of taxes or penalties keep you from either opening a 529 or from withdrawing from it when you need to.

Student Account Owners

Most of the time, the account owner is the parent or maybe a grandparent or other relative. But sometimes the account owner is the student. Typical scenarios may include:

- A student whose parents are either unwilling or unable to shoulder education expenses. In this case, it makes sense for the student to use a 529 if there's a state tax break.

- Parents who are contributing to their student's education but want their student to be responsible for their own educational expenses.

If this is your situation, be aware of the following:

- Of the states that provide a tax break for contributions, many only give the account owner the tax break when they contribute to their own account. In these states, neither the parent nor the student will receive the tax break when the parent is the one who contributes to an account owned by the student.

- Whether the parent or the dependent student owns the account, there's no difference in financial aid eligibility. Student-owned 529s are counted as if the parent owned them.

Rolling Over a 529 Account

You can move your money from one plan to another plan through a process called a rollover. Possible reasons why you would roll over your 529 include:

- You moved and your new home state provides a tax break for rollovers and you either didn't receive a tax break for your previous contributions or it was less than the tax break offered by your new state.

- You are no longer happy with your current plan and you want to move to a better plan. This may be because of high fees, poor performance, or a poor experience.

Warning: If you previously received a state tax break on your original contributions, you may be required to pay the tax break back if you roll over to another state's plan. Your new home state may or may not provide a tax break for rollovers to balance out the clawback. If your new state's tax break for rollovers is more than the tax break in your previous home state, it probably makes sense to roll it over.

Otherwise, consider opening a new account for your future contributions and don't roll over your old account.

Rollovers come in two flavors:

- **Trustee-to-trustee rollover:** Also called a direct rollover, trustee-to-trustee rollovers are the simplest. You submit your request either online or through the mail, providing instructions about your rollover. Your new plan will then contact your current plan and transfer the money with little or no involvement from you. It generally takes a week or two for the money to be transferred.

- **Indirect rollover:** In this scenario, you request a withdrawal from your old plan and they send you a check. You have 60 days to deposit the check into another 529 plan. If you don't do it within 60 days, you'll be subject to federal tax and a 10% penalty on the earnings portion of the withdrawal.

Each plan specifies its own rollover process. With some plans it's as simple as submitting a form, while other plans require safeguards such as a notary signature or a medallion signature guarantee to prevent unauthorized transfers.[1]

Here are some additional things to consider when rolling over a 529 account:

- You can only roll over once per beneficiary in any 12-month period. If you roll over more times than this, you'll owe federal income tax and a 10% penalty on the earnings portion of the rollover.

- Your current plan and/or your new plan may charge a fee for the rollover.

- If your current plan is a prepaid tuition plan, your prepaid credits will be cashed out, possibly unfavorably.

Rolling a 529 into an ABLE Account

In 2014, Congress created the Achieving a Better Life Experience (ABLE) account. ABLE accounts are designed to help disabled individuals and families cope with the additional expense of living with a major disability. If your beneficiary qualifies and you have a 529 account with a disabled beneficiary, then you may be able to roll over your 529 into an ABLE account.

Things to be aware of:

- The onset of the disability must be prior to age 26.[2]

- Unless Congress amends the law, the rollover must happen before January 1, 2026.

- Contributions to ABLE accounts have an annual contribution cap (e.g., $16,000 in 2022) and rollovers from 529s into an ABLE account count toward the cap.

- If the beneficiary uses Medicaid, Medicaid can clawback money from an ABLE account when the beneficiary dies. Medicaid can't take money from a 529.

- A disabled beneficiary is an exception to the 10% penalty for non-eligible distributions from a 529. The beneficiary will need to pay income tax on the earnings portion of any distribution, but it's likely they'll owe zero tax.

- Your home state may recapture any previous tax break when you roll over.

With no penalty and minimal taxes when distributing to a disabled beneficiary, it makes little sense to roll a 529 into an ABLE account.

Roll Over U.S. Savings Bonds to 529 Accounts

If you want to use either Series EE or Series I Savings Bonds to pay for college, you may be able to avoid paying tax on the earnings by rolling them into a 529 account.

Things to keep in mind:

- Your modified adjusted gross income (MAGI) must be less than $100,800 (in 2022; $158,650 if married filing jointly). If you expect your future income to exceed these limits, consider rolling the bonds into a 529 sooner, rather than later.

- When you file your income tax return, you'll tell the IRS about the rollover by marking "QTP" on Form 8815.[3] This is the same form that you'd file if using the savings bonds to pay for tuition or to roll them into a Coverdell ESA.

- Tax-free rollovers are limited to the taxpayer, the taxpayer's spouse, or a dependent. This can be a problem for grandparents wanting to gift savings bonds to a grandchild. One possible workaround is to first roll the bonds into a 529 with the taxpayer as beneficiary, and then roll over that 529 into a 529 with the target student as beneficiary.

- Saving bonds can only be used for tuition and fees. By rolling the bonds into a 529, you give yourself the ability to use the money for room and board, books, supplies, and computer equipment.

Roll Over a Coverdell ESA to a 529

One of the drawbacks of a Coverdell ESA is that you must use all of it by the time the beneficiary turns 30. One escape hatch is rolling the ESA into a 529.[4] Rolling an ESA into a 529 counts as a qualified expense. Things to consider:

- There is no limit on the number of trustee-to-trustee rollovers from ESAs to 529s.

- The ESA rollover must be into a 529 for the same beneficiary.

- Your rollover won't count toward your annual gift tax exclusion limits, because the original contributions to the ESA were already subject to the gift tax.

- This is a one-way street: you cannot roll a 529 into an ESA.

Changing Beneficiaries

If you no longer need your 529, don't worry. A great option is to change the beneficiary to another student. Here are some things to consider:

- Changing beneficiaries doesn't have the same 12-month restriction as do rollovers for the same beneficiary. In fact, changing beneficiaries back-and-forth is a way you can legally get around the 12-month restriction on rollovers (see above).

- Your new beneficiary must be a family member of the current beneficiary. Family members include the beneficiary's:

  - Spouse

- Descendant

- Brother, sister, stepbrother, or stepsister

- Father or mother, or one of their ancestors

- Stepfather or stepmother

- Niece or nephew

- Aunt or uncle

- Father-in-law, mother-in-law, brother-in-law, or sister-in-law

- A spouse of any of the above, and

- Any first cousin.

- If your new beneficiary is of a lower generation than the original beneficiary (e.g., a child of the beneficiary, a niece/nephew), then you'll trigger the Generation Skipping Transfer Tax (GSTT). If the new beneficiary is of the same generation (e.g., spouse, sibling of the beneficiary, first cousin) or a higher generation (e.g., parent, grandparent, aunt, or uncle), then you should be okay. I will cover the GSTT later in this chapter.

- Remember, there is no deadline on when you must use the money in your 529. You can keep the account around indefinitely. Maybe your student will go to graduate school later in life. Or maybe you could use a future grandchild as a beneficiary.

Account Owner Changes

Some plans allow changing the account owner. For some plans, it's as simple as filling out a form and mailing it in. However, other states limit account ownership changes to all but a few unusual circumstances, such as the death or incapacitation of the current owner.

If you live in a state that has restrictions, you could roll over the account into another state's plan that does allow changes in account owner. However, your home state may expect you to pay back some of the tax break that you previously received.

Gift Tax and Generation Skipping Transfer Tax

Contributions to a 529 are considered gifts and are included in the annual gift tax limit of $16,000 (in 2022). The gift tax limits how much one individual can give to another without the giver reporting the gift to the IRS.

A related tax is the generation skipping transfer tax (GSTT). This tax applies when a donor skips a generation in making a gift that exceeds the annual limit.[5] The GSTT prevents wealthy grandparents from avoiding the gift tax twice by skipping their children and giving directly to their grandchildren.

For most families, the gift tax and the GSTT are only annoyances. Avoiding them might be important if:

- You want to avoid complications when filing your income tax return. Even if you end up paying no tax, exceeding the annual gift tax limit means filing an additional form.[6]

- You are worried that you will exceed the lifetime gift tax exemption.[7]

You can avoid these taxes by keeping annual contributions to the same beneficiary under the annual limit of $16,000 (in 2022).

> **Example:** Elise opens a 529 for her granddaughter. To avoid triggering the gift tax and dipping into her lifetime exclusion amount, she splits her $20,000 contribution between two years, contributing $16,000 the first year, and $4,000 the second year.

If you're married, you and your spouse can both give separate gifts, totaling $32,000 per year. Because some states only give tax breaks to account owners, you may need to open two separate accounts to maximize the state tax break.

The gift tax can also apply when changing a beneficiary. If the new beneficiary is of the same generation (or higher) as the current beneficiary, then no gift tax is due.

> **Example:** Elise's grandson recently graduated from college and her 529 still contains $25,460. She rolls over the account to a 529 for a granddaughter. Even though they aren't brother and sister, Elise avoids the gift tax because the beneficiaries are in the same generation.

If you trigger either the gift tax or the GSTT, be aware that it's the donor of the gift that pays the tax, not the recipient. Because these taxes can be tricky, you should check with your tax advisor.

Superfunding a 529

Superfunding a 529 is an exception to the gift tax rules. Superfunding involves bunching together up to five years of contributions into a single year. Through superfunding, you can contribute up to $80,000 (5 years x $16,000, in 2022) to a 529 before you trigger the gift tax.

Important details:

- If you superfund a 529, you'll need to file Form 709.

- If you die within five years of superfunding, the contribution is prorated over the remaining years, and a portion is included in your overall estate, counting toward your lifetime gift exclusion limit.

- Many states have an upper limit on the annual tax break for 529 contributions in any given year, and not all of these states allow you to carry excess contributions into future tax years. Check your home state's 529 rules to see if you will limit your tax break by superfunding.

Example: As part of her estate planning, Elise contributes $80,000 to a 529 account for her granddaughter. She uses Form 709 to spread the gift across five years. Sadly, Elise dies three years after the superfunding. The prorated contributions for years four and five, or $32,000, are included in her estate toward her lifetime gift tax exemption.

Deducting Losses from Your 529 Account

Depending on your choice of investments and market volatility, your 529 can decline in value. Prior to 2017, taxpayers could claim a loss on their tax return when this occurred. To claim the loss, the account had to be closed and the owner had to account for any distributions. However, in 2017 the law changed and 529 losses can no longer be claimed.[8]

In reality, this change wasn't a big deal for most taxpayers. First, the loss had to be greater than 2% of the taxpayer's

AGI. Second, taking the loss required closing the account. Unless you were actively paying for eligible expenses at the time, closing the account would mean you'd have to pay back any state tax breaks you'd received previously.

Things You Can't Do with Your 529

In addition to the restrictions discussed throughout this book, you can't do the following with your 529:

- **No Using It As Loan Collateral:** You may be able to take a loan from your 401(k) for a down payment on your first home, but you can't do that with your 529.

- **No Stock or Bond Contributions:** You can only contribute cash or cash equivalents to your 529. To contribute either shares of stock or bonds, you'll need to sell them first, then contribute the cash.

- **No Opening an Account for An Unborn Child:** If you're expecting a child, you could open the 529 with yourself as beneficiary, then change beneficiaries once the child is born. See earlier in this chapter for changing beneficiaries.

Summary

If all goes well, you'll never run into any of the scenarios in this chapter. If you do, consult with your tax advisor.

---

[1] https://www.investor.gov/introduction-investing/investing-basics/glossary/medallion-signature-guarantees-preventing

[2] There have been repeated attempts as of 2022 to increase the age of eligibility, but as of 2022, these attempts have not been successful.

[3] QTP is an abbreviation for "qualified tuition program"

[4] Source: https://uscode.house.gov/view.xhtml?req=(title:26%20section:530%20edition:prelim), (2)(B), Qualified education expenses includes contributions to a 529

[5] A generation skip is when the giver is at least 37 ½ years older than the giftee

[6] See Form 709:. https://www.irs.gov/forms-pubs/about-form-709

[7] $12.06 million in 2022. Only when you exceed your lifetime exemption limit do you pay tax on your gift, but it's a steep 40% flat tax on the excessive gift.

[8] Deducting losses from 529s was suspended through 2025

11

Tips and Strategies

The following tips and strategies can save you thousands of dollars as you save for college. Not every tip or strategy applies to every family. I've described when they may or may not apply to you.

Tips for Maximizing Your Federal Tax Savings

- **Save Early to Maximize Tax-Free Growth.** See Chapter 4.

- **Avoid the Gift Tax** if you're married by opening separate 529s. See Chapter 10.

- **Avoid the Generation Skipping Tax** by keeping your contributions below the annual gift tax limit. See Chapter 10.

- **Roll Savings Bonds into a 529** if you want to use the money to pay for room and board or computer equipment. Roll them over before you hit the income limits. See Chapter 10.

- **Reimburse Your Student** instead of yourself when you make a taxable withdrawal. See Chapter 10.

- **Coordinate Withdrawals from Your ESA and 529** to avoid paying income tax and penalties. See Chapter 10.

Tips for Maximizing Your State Tax Savings

- **Contribute to Your Home State Plan** if your state has a tax break. See Chapter 3.

- **Roll Over Your 529 to Your New Home State** if you move and your new state gives a tax break for rollovers. See Chapter 10.

Other Tips and Strategies

- **Choose a 529 with the Lowest Fees** if you either receive no state tax break or if you receive a tax break regardless of which 529 plan you use. See Chapter 3.

- **December Is for Distributions.** Withdraw money at the end of the year to maximize tax-free growth. See Chapter 5.

- **Use Your 529 for Room and Board** if your student attends full time and is not living at home. See Chapter 5.

- **Buy Your Student's Computer** using your 529. See Chapter 5.

- **Pay for Tuition at an International School.** See Chapter 5.

- **Pay for Graduate School.** See Chapter 5.

- **Pay for K-12 Tuition.** See Chapter 9.

- **Pay Off Student Loan Debt.** See Chapter 9.

- **Don't Roll Over a 529 into an ABLE Account.** See Chapter 10.

- **Withdraw Money Penalty-Free** if your student earned a scholarship or grant. See Chapter 6.

- **Change the Account Owner Using a Rollover** if your state prohibits account owner changes. See Chapter 10.

- **Change the Beneficiary** if you have money left over and want to avoid income tax and the penalty. See Chapter 10.

- **Enroll an Unborn Child** by making yourself or another family member the beneficiary. See Chapter 10.

- **Circumvent the Once-Per-12-Month Rollover Limit** by first rolling the account to a new beneficiary. See Chapter 10.

Summary

You're a finisher! Congratulations!

For many students, college provides an opportunity to discover and cultivate who they will be for the rest of their lives. By learning how to use a 529 and striving to overcome the inertia of inaction, you've started on the path to success! I wish you and your student the best on the college adventure.

I want to hear about your 529 experiences. Please send me your feedback at info@529handbook.com or through my website: https://529handbook.com. I look forward to hearing from you.

You can help other readers discover how 529s can help them maximize their college savings by leaving a review of this book.

Scan this QR code to get started:

Additional Resources

The following resources can help you compare 529 plans:

- Nonprofit that publishes 529 plan data and provides planning and comparison tools: https://www.collegesavings.org/

- Independent 529 plan ranking by features and fees: https://www.morningstar.com/articles/1062917/the-top-529-education-savings-plans-of-2021

The following are resources for learning more about tax topics:

- The section of law defining "qualified tuition programs" or 529s: https://uscode.house.gov/view.xhtml?req=(title:26%20section:529%20edition:prelim)

- IRS publication for education tax benefits: https://www.irs.gov/publications/p970

- IRS publication of popular questions and answers about 529 plans: https://www.irs.gov/newsroom/529-plans-questions-and-answers

The following are resources that provide data related to saving for college:

- Statistics about saving for college: https://educationdata.org/college-savings-statistics

- Annual report that examines how families and students pay for college: https://www.salliemae.com/about/leading-research/how-america-pays-for-college/

- Report by the College Board about trends in student aid: https://research.collegeboard.org/trends/student-aid

- Report by the College Board about trends in college prices: https://research.collegeboard.org/trends/college-pricing

- Reporting on the affordability of college: http://collegeaffordability.urban.org/covering-expenses/savings

- Quickly find the Cost of Attendance at different schools: https://collegescorecard.ed.gov/

- Federal Student Aid Estimator: https://studentaid.gov/aid-estimator/

- FAFSA Formulas and Tables for 2022-2023: https://fsapartners.ed.gov/sites/default/files/2021-08/2223EFCFormulaGuide.pdf

These are other resources that you might find helpful or interesting:

- Calculate how much I should save for college: https://www.fedfinancial.org/calculator/how-much-should-i-save-college

- Investor information about Coverdell ESAs: https://www.finra.org/investors/learn-to-invest/types-investments/saving-for-education/esa-and-custodial-accounts

- Historic 529 plan data: https://www.federalreserve.gov/releases/efa/efa-project-section-529-college-plans.htm

Made in United States
Troutdale, OR
07/05/2023

10990503R00086